A VOICE
in the
WILDERNESS

GOD'S PRESENCE
IN YOUR
DESERT PLACES

CHARLES H. DYER

MOODY PUBLISHERS
CHICAGO

© 2004 by

CHARLES H. DYER

Library of Congress Cataloging-in-Publication Data

Dyer, Charles H., 1952-
   A voice in the wilderness : God's presence in your desert places /
   Charles H. Dyer.
      p. cm.
   ISBN 0-8024-2908-4
   1. Consolation. 2. Bible. O.T. Isaiah XL, 3-31--Criticism,
   interpretation, etc. I. Title.

   BV4905.3.D94 2004
   224'.106--dc22

                                                    2004010479

1 3 5 7 9 10 8 6 4 2

to Greg and Lisa Hatteberg,

who model the sufficiency of God's grace.

All who know you are blessed.

Contents

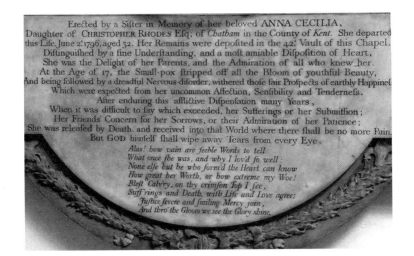

Erected by a Sister in Memory of her beloved ANNA CECILIA,
Daughter of CHRISTOPHER RHODES Efq; of *Chatham* in the County of *Kent*. She departed
this Life June 2ᵈ 1796, aged 32. Her Remains were depofited in the 42ᵈ Vault of this Chapel.
Diftinguifhed by a fine Underftanding, and a moft amiable Difpofition of Heart,
She was the Delight of her Parents, and the Admiration of all who knew her.
At the Age of 17, the Small-pox ftripped off all the Bloom of youthful Beauty,
And being followed by a dreadful Nervous-diforder, withered thofe fair Profpeᶜts of earthly Happinefs
Which were expecᶜted from her uncommon Affecᶜtion, Senfibility and Tendernefs.
After enduring this afflicᶜtive Difpenfation many Years,
When it was difficult to fay which exceeded, her Sufferings or her Submiffion;
Her Friends' Concern for her Sorrows, or their Admiration of her Patience;
She was releafed by Death. and received into that World where there fhall be no more Pain,
But GOD himfelf fhall wipe away Tears from every Eye.

Alas! how vain are feeble Words to tell
What once fhe was, and why I lov'd fo well:
None elfe but he who form'd the Heart can know
How great her Worth, or how extreme my Woe!
Bleft Calv'ry, on thy crimfon Top I fee,
Suff'rings and Death, with Life and Love agree;
Juftice fevere and fmiling Mercy join,
And thro' the Gloom we see the Glory fhine.

Introduction

London's Victoria and Albert Museum is Britain's equivalent of Grandma's attic. The building houses a hodgepodge of odds and ends collected by Queen Victoria and her husband when they ruled an empire that circled the globe. Massive hand-carved chairs sit next to delicate pieces of porcelain. Graceful statues stare out at grotesque wax carvings of graves and ghosts. The outlandish mix of art and artifacts gives the entire museum a quirky, Dr. Seuss-like quality.

Wedged among the thousands of gifts is an unusual plaque that originally hung in a church in London. The plaque, with its ornate carving, is displayed in the sculpture wing of the museum because it was sculpted by John Bacon the Younger. Few stop to look at the plaque. Even less take the time to decipher its Old English script, with its *s*'s written like *f*'s. But those who do read it discover a poignant tale of sorrow and love.

The benefactor commissioned the plaque and had it placed in the chapel to memorialize her sister, Anna Cecilia Rhodes. Anna was born in 1764 and died in 1796 at the age of thirty-two. A life cut short by death is indeed sad. But the last half of Anna's short life was marred by personal pain. When she was just seventeen, this beautiful young woman contracted smallpox. And quoting from the plaque, the disease "stripped off all the bloom of youthful beauty." Her loss of physical beauty was "followed by a dreadful nervous disorder" that "withered those fair prospects of earthly happiness."

Physical deformity. Emotional heartache. A life cut short by death. One senses the suffering and sadness that seemed to squeeze this young woman in its viselike grip. Where does someone go for answers when life punches them in the gut, knocking them to their knees? Amid the ashes of personal tragedy, how can an individual rediscover meaning and purpose for life?

We have no direct answer from Anna, but her sister opened her heart in a closing poem to share her source of comfort and hope. Anna's sister, in spite of her tears, found inner strength through her knowledge of the nature and character of God. Read—and reflect—on the words she had carved into the bottom of the plaque:

> Alas! how vain are feeble Words to tell
> What once she was, and why I lov'd so well;
> > None else but he who form'd the Heart can know
> > How great her Worth, or how extreme my Woe!
> > Blest Calv'ry, on thy crimson Top I see,
> > Suff'rings and Death, with Life and Love agree;
> Justice severe and smiling Mercy join,
> And thro' the Gloom we see the Glory shine.

Whatever your burden, whatever your discouragement, whatever your loss, God stands ready to comfort you in your greatest hour of need. "He who form'd the Heart" does indeed know—deeply and intimately—your personal struggles and pain. My prayer is that this book will take you on a journey of comfort and hope so that "thro' the Gloom" you may be able to "see the Glory shine."

I can trace the beginning of this book back to a personal wilderness experience about ten years ago. My dad had to enter a hospital for heart bypass surgery, and I flew home to Pennsylvania to be with my mom. The surgery was successful, but his recovery did not go as well as planned. For several days Mom and I sat in the waiting room while Dad struggled to recover. Between the short visits in the intensive care unit (ICU), we had a lot of time to sit . . . and think.

Those were difficult days, but I discovered two anchors that kept me from being tossed about spiritually and emotionally. The first was God's Word, especially the comfort I received from Isaiah 40. God's promises were tested, and they were found to be true. I had always appreciated Isaiah 40, but during those troubling times it became God's personal message of hope for me.

The second anchor was the encouragement of God's people. The pastor from my parents' church, along with a number of other friends and neighbors, stopped by to talk and pray. And they were a great encouragement. Their visits were not long, but they were long remembered.

At the time of Dad's surgery I was working at Dallas Theological Seminary under President Chuck Swindoll. I say that to help explain two other significant events God used to encourage me during this time. The first happened during one of our early visits to ICU following surgery. As we walked past the nurses' station, a nurse called out to me, "Oh, your doctor in Dallas called to check up on your dad!"

I had no idea what physician from Dallas even knew I was in Pennsylvania, so I asked the nurse, "What was his name?"

"Oh," she said, "it was a Doctor Swindoll."

That brought a needed smile to our faces!

Then, when Dad finally recovered enough to leave ICU, I returned to Dallas. When I got back to my office at the seminary, I found a note on my desk. It was a simple note from Chuck, written in his own distinctive handwriting. His short message overwhelmed me with its love and concern. That note, in its tattered envelope, remains one of my most cherished possessions.

> *My Dear Friend:*
>
> *You have been through a long and lonely journey these past several days. I understand. I've been there with my dad.*
>
> *So many, many times you have come to my mind. Each time I've sent a word upward . . . and sensed the reassurance that "Our God is in the heavens . . . He has done what pleases Him."*
>
> *We're all grateful your father is enjoying such a remarkable recovery. What a great feeling is* relief! *With a smile that says, "Welcome back."*
>
> *Chuck*

God's Word . . . and the comforting words of God's people. Together they link arms to support us through life's struggles. The goal of this book is to bring these two elements together in a way that will comfort and encourage you. Much of the book will focus on Isaiah 40, that grand message of comfort that meant so much to me in my time of need.

But as you read through the pages of this book, you will also meet other pilgrims who have traversed that winding pathway leading through life's wilderness. These men and women —whom I know and love—have paused in their own spiritual journey long enough to write a personal "postcard from the wilderness." Each reflection is as uniquely personal as its author. As you read them you will come to appreciate these fellow travelers as friends, guides, mentors—and, most of all, as encouragers.

Their individual circumstances vary, yet a common thread links each postcard. That thread is God's grace and comfort that each experienced during a particularly difficult time in his or her life.

As you read their accounts, my prayer is that you will also gain greater insight into the reality of God's sustaining grace. May God use their words—and His Word of comfort in Isaiah 40—to encourage you in your journey through this wilderness we call life.

Chapter One

Comfort amid the Sand, Sweat, and Blood of Our Lives

I sat near the back of the church, waiting for the wake to begin. I was there to honor a friend whose wife had suddenly and unexpectedly died. But what could I say — or do — to comfort a grieving husband?

The answer came when the pastor asked the congregation to rise as he led the family up the aisle . . . quoting Scripture after Scripture that focused on God's sustaining comfort.

"Yea, though I walk through the valley of the shadow of death . . . thou art with me."

"In my Father's house are many mansions. . . . I go to prepare a place for you. And if I go and prepare a place for you, I will come again, and receive you unto myself; that where I am, there ye may be also."

"I will lift up mine eyes unto the hills, from whence cometh my help. My help cometh from the Lord, which made heaven and earth."[1]

The Bible offers eternal answers to life's troubling questions. But are those answers relevant to us today? The images in the Bible make clear this is not a sterile Book immaculately conceived in some sort of mystical, holy vacuum. Though God *is* the ultimate Author, He used human writers as His instruments. And both they and the Lord speak through varied images of the day: the caring shepherd (Psalm 23; John 10:1–15), a shield and horn (Psalm 18:2; 112:9), and a mother hen (Matthew 23:37), to name a few. To interpret His Word properly we must enter their world. The bleating of sheep on barren hills, the mournful wail of a ram's-horn trumpet on the temple steps, or the harsh clang of sword hitting sword in epic battle hang like tapestries in the background of nearly every page.

To understand Israel's struggle in the wilderness, we must smell the dust kicked up by the murmuring multitude's sandals and feel the sweat falling from their sun-scorched foreheads as they desperately search for water in a parched desert. Or to understand the fear of Jesus' disciples, we must hear the waves crashing over the bow of the boat and feel the sting of the wind-whipped spray on their faces as they strain against the oars, struggling to survive a late-night storm on the Sea of Galilee.

The harsh conditions of that time may seem remote— few of us ply the lake or ocean for a living; even fewer live in the desert. Yet at times we face hardships just as fierce and challenging as people living in the days of Moses, Isaiah, or Jesus. And the Scriptures of that day speak to our hardships as loudly as they did to Israel's challenges more than two millennia ago. So to understand our day, and Isaiah's writing, let's first review the historical background, which provides texture, color, and depth to the biblical account. The words will take on greater force and impact when we see with increased clarity their connection to the real world in which we live.

Assyria's Invasion of Judah

The background to Isaiah 40 includes the sounds of several thousand snorting horses pushing wildly against their yokes, their hooves pounding into the dry Judean ground, nostrils flaring, ears attuned to the crack of the chariot drivers' whips. As these panting steeds race by, their sound subsides, only to be replaced by the deep, rhythmic thump of 200,000 soldiers' leather sandals marching along the hard-packed road.

The smoke of burning cities and towns mixes with the dust kicked up by the thousands of refugees fleeing from the invading Assyrian army, seeking safety and security in Jerusalem. The scene is one of confusion, fear, and, at times, even panic.

Inside Jerusalem, the streets are filling with refugees from every corner of the land. Crying babies reach out to mothers who are so distracted by dark thoughts of impending destruction that they scarcely notice. Food and water are already in short supply, and the situation deteriorates daily as frightened civilians continue to pour through the city's gates. Rumors spread as the people quiz each new arrival. Where have they come from? What have they seen? What have they heard from others?

Tension mounts as each new report brings the Assyrian army ever closer. The rising plume of dust from the village of

Nob, on the northern edge of the Mount of Olives, confirms their worst fears. The Assyrians have reached the outskirts of Jerusalem! Then a shout is heard from the watchman on the city's southern wall. A column of Assyrian soldiers is also making its way up the road from Bethlehem! The city is surrounded; all avenues of escape have been cut off. Acting on instinct, a large crowd rushes toward the temple to cry out to God for deliverance.

Words of Deliverance

Pushing his way through the people, the prophet Isaiah forces his way to the front of the panic-stricken crowd. The people grow quiet as Isaiah begins to speak. Boldly he announces God's protection and deliverance for those hiding behind Jerusalem's walls: The Assyrian king "will not enter this city or shoot an arrow here. He will not come before it with shield or build a siege ramp against it" (Isaiah 37:33). The words sound almost too good to be true, but the prophet assures the people that God's deliverance will come soon.

Isaiah's words barely have enough time to reach the ears of everyone in Jerusalem before God brings them to pass. In a single night God strikes down 185,000 Assyrian solders. "So Sennacherib king of Assyria broke camp and withdrew" (verses 36–37).

Jerusalem was spared! God answered prayer! King Hezekiah and the people of Jerusalem experienced a genuine miracle. They had the biblical equivalent of a mountaintop experience. Unfortunately, when you walk off a mountaintop, you are usually heading toward a valley.

Some time after the Assyrian army retreated from Jerusalem, an envoy arrived from the king of Babylon bringing gifts for Hezekiah. Word of Hezekiah's miraculous recovery from physical illness—and, no doubt, his victory over the Assyrians—had reached Babylon's king, who was also struggling against the Assyrians. Perhaps Hezekiah would share the secret of his great victory. But instead of pointing the visitors toward the great God of Israel, King Hezekiah basked in their praise and "showed them what was in his storehouses—the silver, the gold, the spices, the fine oil, his entire armory and everything found among his treasures. There was nothing in his palace or in all his kingdom that Hezekiah did not show them" (39:2). Hezekiah foolishly took credit for a victory he had not won.

Hezekiah had feared the Assyrians, but it was the Babylonians who would become Judah's ultimate enemy. God sent Isaiah to announce the grim news. "The time will surely come when everything in your palace, and all that your fathers have stored up until this day, will be carried off to Babylon. Nothing will be left" (verse 6). The predicted invasion didn't take place for another century, but it *did* come. Long after Isaiah had died, God sent King Nebuchadnezzar of Babylon against Jerusalem to fulfill this prophecy.

In 586 B.C. Nebuchadnezzar's army entered Jerusalem. The soldiers sacked and burned God's temple that had been built by Solomon. They captured Judah's king as he tried to escape. Blinded and bound in chains, he was carried into captivity in Babylon where he eventually died. Most of the other inhabitants of Jerusalem who survived the brutal siege were also carried off into captivity.

Defeated. Disheartened. Depressed. Distressed in spirit. Deported from their homeland to a foreign country. These were the people who had looked for the light at the end of a dark tunnel—only to discover that it was the lamp of the onrushing train of God's judgment bearing down on them. And the impact was horrific.

God's Program of Comfort

God's judgment through the Babylonian army may have taken the people of Judah by surprise in 586 B.C., but the prophet Isaiah had clearly seen it coming. He not only announced the event long before it took place, he also wrote a message of comfort and hope to those who would endure this time of national tragedy. Isaiah 39 predicted Jerusalem's fall; Isaiah 40 offers comfort to those affected by that fall.

Indeed, more than a century before the event even happened, God boldly announced His plan to provide comfort for those who would experience the approaching pain and sorrow. "Comfort, comfort my people, says your God. Speak tenderly to Jerusalem" (40:1–2a). The remainder of Isaiah 40 contains God's prescription for healing Jerusalem's pain and discouragement—for providing comfort in times of sorrow.

But what does the message of Isaiah 40 have to do with you? Can words that were written 2,700 years ago make a difference in your life today? They can, even though your circumstances will not match those of ancient Israel. The people of Israel experienced the loss of national identity and personal liberty. They saw their God-ordained religious and civil institutions crumble. They watched helplessly as loved ones died of starvation and disease. They saw friends and family members raped, tortured, and murdered by brutal soldiers. They felt their throats tighten from thirst as they endured a forced march into a strange land where they became slaves.

Our individual circumstances are not the same, but we have all experienced personal heartache and trauma. Perhaps you are struggling with the loss of a loved one—the sorrow and intense loneliness pulling you down into a black pit of despair. Or perhaps you have been seared by the hot iron of rejection—the hurt and anger burning your soul, leaving a wound that refuses to heal. Maybe you are facing physical or emotional pain that has turned your life upside down and left you feeling violated, vulnerable, and valueless.

It is even possible that you do not even know exactly why you feel so lonely and discouraged. Others might think you are happy and content, but your smile is nothing more than a mask that hides your deep personal sadness.

The causes for sorrow and discouragement vary, but the results are the same.

Are you discouraged? If you are, then walk with me through the majestic landscape of Isaiah 40 to discover God's sustaining comfort.

As you do, along the way through the desert experiences, you will encounter oases that refresh, even as the nine men and women who have written their "Postcards from the Wilderness." The first postcard comes from a seasoned Pennsylvania pastor, who found comfort during his own "dark hour."

"Your daughter has achondroplasia—she's a dwarf."

Those were the words of the head of the genetics department, who, with other doctors, had been examining our infant daughter, Anna, who had developed a high fever within eleven days of birth. My wife, Barb, had the presence of mind to ask the doctor pertinent questions. I just stood there silent—and numb.

Barb spent the night in the hospital with little Anna—as she had been doing each night—while I drove home in the darkness. The phone rang soon after I walked through the front door. I picked up the receiver and heard the familiar voice of Dr. Harry Fletcher, president of the college where I was teaching. Harry was the man who had led me to the Lord.

Harry tenderly asked about Anna. I told him of her condition. He expressed his concern, and then we hung up. Minutes later the doorbell rang. I opened the door and there stood Harry! He hugged me and quoted Exodus 4:11 (NASB): "Who has made man's mouth? Or who makes him mute or deaf, or seeing or blind? Is it not I, the Lord?"

Harry reminded me that God formed Anna the way He desired and that He could be trusted to do what was best. He then prayed briefly and left. "Indeed, Lord," I prayed, "You don't make mistakes."

Later that evening I wrote Anna in the margin of my Bible at Exodus 4:11. Soon peace and comfort replaced the gloom and despair. A few days later my son Joel and I brought Barb and Anna home. Today Anna is a vibrant teenager who loves God and walks closely to Him.

I thank God for sending a close, personal friend to encourage me in my darkest hour. God is faithful and unchanging.

Douglas Lyon, pastor
Shiloh Bible Church, Bloomsburg, Pennsylvania

Postcards from the Wilderness

Postcards from the Wilderness

Postcards from the Wilder

Postcards from the Wilderness

Chapter Two

The Comfort of God's Presence

Isaiah 40:3–5

One of the special joys of Christmas is the sound of holiday music. Certain songs stir up memories and emotions that carry us back to our childhood. Songs like "I'm Dreaming of a White Christmas" may evoke memories of laughter at long-forgotten family gatherings, sledding with friends through newly fallen snow, or the delicious smell of hot chocolate simmering on the stove.

But some of our most memorable songs are Christmas carols—melodies whose words are rooted in the Bible and Christian tradition that focus on the birth of Jesus in Bethlehem. The strains of "Silent Night," "Joy to the World," and "O Come, All Ye Faithful" help us push aside the crass commercialization of Christmas. They remind us anew that the true purpose for the holiday is to remember the first coming of God's Son . . . even as we look forward to His return.

In many communities the Christmas season is also the time to attend a performance of Handel's *Messiah*, one of the grandest examples of Scripture set to music. Following the overture, the words of Isaiah 40:1–4 reach out to pull the audience into the scriptural procession that winds its way from the Cross to the Crown.

Comfort ye, comfort ye my people, saith your God.
Speak ye comfortably to Jerusalem,
And cry unto her, that her warfare is accomplished,
that her iniquity is pardoned.
The voice of him that crieth in the wilderness,
Prepare ye the way of the Lord,
Make straight in the desert a highway for our God.

Every valley shall be exalted, and every mountain
and hill made low;
The crooked straight, and the rough places plain.[1]

The Wilderness of Judah

Isaiah's words of comfort and hope, penned seven centuries before the birth of Israel's Messiah, found their fulfillment in the ministry of John the Baptist in the wilderness of Judah. In his powerful prophetic voice, John announced to the people of Jerusalem, "I am the voice of one calling in the desert, 'Make straight the way for the Lord' " (John 1:23). He was, ultimately, the messenger sent by God to prepare Judah for the arrival of her Messiah.

But move back in history to a time hundreds of years before the beginning of John the Baptist's ministry or the birth of Jesus. Entering a small home, your eyes strain to adjust to the dark interior. Eventually you can see well enough to make out a group of Jewish refugees seated around a small wooden table. Spread out across the table is an old scroll. Peering at the scroll through the dim light of the flickering oil lamp, these captives in Babylon read with amazement the words of the prophet Isaiah. The scroll is over a century old, yet the words are so relevant it's as if they had been penned only yesterday.

As the captives read the scroll, they think about all the pain and heartache they have experienced. Their ancestral homes are now nothing more than piles of broken stones, covered with thistles and thorns, inhabited only by lizards and rock badgers. Family tombs that once held the remains of loved ones now lie open and neglected. Solomon's temple, the holy site where they went to worship God, is now a blackened shell, the heat from the burning cedarwood crumbling the limestone blocks into lime. They frown as they think about the temple's shattered stones standing in silent witness to God's judgment of their nation's idolatry.

As they read Isaiah's prediction of Judah's captivity in Babylon, they understand all too well what the prophet was announcing. Their past glory is only a memory, their present life is nothing more than endless days of hard service in a strange land, and their future is shrouded in uncertainty. Or so it seems.

Comfort Within the Wilderness

Then they come to words almost too wonderful to read . . . words of comfort to those living in great discouragement. But how was such comfort possible? What could possibly happen that could turn their cries of pain into shouts of joy?

The arrival of God's comfort would be announced by His messenger in the wilderness. The wilderness! As the exiles read these words of promise, they understand immediately the picture being painted by Isaiah. The wilderness being described is the wilderness of Judah just to the east of Jerusalem. Starting on the eastern slopes of the Mount of Olives, it twists its way down into the Jordan Valley, running along the entire length of the Dead Sea.

The Rugged Judean Wilderness

This is not a wilderness of sand, like the Sahara Desert. Nor is it a flat, empty expanse that stretches off into the horizon like some other deserts. The Judean wilderness is rough and rugged, a land of deep, twisting gorges carved into chalky limestone. The ground is hard, harsh, and unyielding. Patches of brown and black flint sprinkled across the surface seem to provide the only variations in color.

The Judean wilderness is a stark metaphor of permanence. Its foreboding hills stood guard when Abraham first entered the land. The same hills watched Joshua lead his army on a daring night march from Gilgal to Gibeon. They saw David flee from Jerusalem toward the Jordan River to escape the evil plans of his own son Absalom. And they watched Satan tempt Jesus, as he enticed the Son of

God to turn the ever-present stones into loaves of bread. The wilderness *never* seemed to change.

The captives in Babylon felt that their spiritual condition matched the physical condition of the wilderness. They were spiritually dry, exiled from God's source of blessing, and surrounded by deep chasms of trouble and difficulty that seemed to make any restoration impossible. And their spiritual condition, like the physical condition of the Judean wilderness, appeared to be permanent. Or was it?

God's Messenger of Hope

Isaiah introduced a messenger who would be the harbinger of change. Imagine the scene pictured by the prophet. Off in the distance, beyond a field of rocks that shimmer from the heat radiating off them, a faint sound is heard. Heads cock forward and eyes scan the horizon to find the source for the sound. Soon a tiny speck appears over a distant hill. As the shape draws closer, it takes on a human form. The faint sound becomes a voice, and eventually the words being spoken by this desert traveler become distinct. "In the desert prepare the way for the LORD; make straight in the wilderness a highway for our God" (Isaiah 40:3). Who is this?

Throughout the ancient Near East, kings would send out messengers to announce their coming. These heralds would go to the cities soon to be visited by the rulers and tell the inhabitants to prepare for the king's arrival. The roadway into town needed to be smoothed out. Its oxcart-rutted tracks had to be filled in. And the stones that had worked their way to the surface had to be thrown off to the side. The town officials would prepare the roadway and then stand ready to offer the monarch the hospitality of the town.

The imagery described by Isaiah was familiar to his readers, but the place and the person must have surprised them. The messenger predicted by the prophet was not coming merely to announce the arrival of a king. He would come to announce the arrival of the King of Kings! And God was coming not to visit monarchs in their grand palaces. Instead, He was coming to give comfort to a beleaguered and distressed people trapped in a wilderness of hopelessness and despair.

Normally, it was the responsibility of the people to prepare the way for the king. They were to fill in the ruts and remove the rocks from the roadway. But the "ruts" in the wilderness of Judah were deep, serpentine valleys, and the "bumps" were thousands of mountains and hills. The "stones" that made the way rough were millions upon millions of sharp flint rocks and large limestone boulders. This was an impossible task for the discouraged remnant. God might be coming, but the obstacles remained.

Changing the Unchangeable

And then the prophet reversed the rules! God Himself would change the unchangeable. "Every valley shall be raised up, every mountain and hill made low; the rough ground shall become level, the rugged places a plain" (verse 4). In the Judean wilderness the valleys never seem to change. They have *always* been obstacles. And the mountains and hills have *always* stood as silent sentinels guarding the ascent to Jerusalem from the east, blocking the pathway into the hills of Judah. And the sharp flint stones that cut into the soles of sandals along with the limestone rocks that make it so easy to slip or to twist an ankle have *always* made walking through the wilderness a treacherous journey.

Isaiah boldly announced that when God comes to rescue His people, no obstacle will be able to stand in His way. What appears to be a problem for us is not a problem for Him. God specializes in eliminating *every* valley and *every* mountain, including those that seem so powerful or permanent we cannot even begin to imagine how they can be overcome.

The prophet looked beyond Judah's temporary trouble to see God's ultimate triumph. "And the glory of the Lord will be revealed, and all mankind together will see it. For the mouth of the Lord has spoken" (verse 5). Isaiah offered comfort through the promise of God's presence. Those who were discouraged could look beyond their circumstances and focus instead on the reality of God's comforting presence. He had not abandoned them. And His coming deliverance was certain, because God Himself was the one making the promise.

Staying Focused on God

We can become discouraged when we focus so intently on our problems that we forget God's presence by our side. Like Peter trying to walk on top of the wind-whipped waves on the Sea of Galilee, we can survive life's storms as long as we keep our focus on the Lord. But all too often we take our eyes off Him and find ourselves sinking into a sea of despair, discouragement, and doubt. Thankfully, Jesus reaches out His hand to us, just as He did to Peter, to catch us before we go completely under (see Matthew 14:28–31). No valley is too deep, no mountain too high—or no sea too tempestuous —to keep God from coming to our rescue.

Are you burdened by problems that seem overwhelming? Perhaps you feel alone in life's harsh wilderness—hemmed in on all sides by mountainous problems and valleys of despair. Or perhaps you feel as if you are drowning in a sea of troubles, struggling helplessly against the doubt and discouragement that threaten to engulf you. Whichever metaphor describes your current struggles, you must realize now that you are not alone. God has promised to come to your aid, bringing comfort and hope.

Look beyond the problems, and understand that no obstacle is too great to keep God from entering into your life.

Years ago Helen Lemmel wrote a simple hymn that captures the truth of these first few verses in Isaiah 40. However dark your circumstances may be, take comfort in the fact that God has not—and never will—abandon you.

O soul, are you weary and troubled?
No light in the darkness you see?
There's light for a look at the Savior,
And life more abundant and free!
Turn your eyes upon Jesus,
Look full in His wonderful face;
And the things of earth will grow strangely dim
In the light of His glory and grace.[2]

"I don't know what to do! I am about ready to give up!"

The lady sat in my office in tears. Her marriage had crumbled.

Obviously she faced a number of serious issues and had come to me for help. Still, I sensed her most pressing need was hope and genuine encouragement.

What I offered were words from Isaiah 40, to " 'comfort, O comfort My people,' says your God. . . . "Clear the way for the Lord in the wilderness; make smooth in the desert a highway for our God. Let every valley be lifted up, and every mountain and hill be made low; and let the rough ground become a plain, and the rugged terrain a broad valley' " (NASB).

On my desk is a rock from the Judean wilderness. Its sharp, uneven edges speak of the harshness of that rugged region. When I hold it, I remember the power of God's promise to smooth out the rough ground of our lives and make them into a broad valley. God takes what looks like an impossible mountain peak and makes a smooth path through the valley.

Over time, He did just that for the woman in my office, her heart rubbed raw from the jagged edge of a divorce. He will do the same for you too, if you'll trust Him.

Doug Cecil, director of alumni and church relations
Dallas Theological Seminary, Dallas, Texas

Postcards from the Wilderness

Chapter Three

The Comfort of God's Promise

Isaiah 40:6–8

*I*n the summer of 2002, Chicago's Museum of Science and Industry hosted a special exhibit on the RMS Titanic, the "unsinkable" cruise ship that sunk on its maiden voyage. The opulent Titanic, costing $1.5 million in 1912 dollars, struck a large iceberg about 350 miles southeast of Newfoundland, Canada, taking more than 1,500 passengers to a watery grave.[1] Since 1987, more than six thousand artifacts have been found. Many of these were displayed at "Titanic: The Exhibition" in Chicago.

Museum guests walked through artifacts arranged in "rooms" that helped the visitors imagine how the items would have been used on the Titanic's fateful maiden voyage. A section of the Titanic's hull captured some of the enormity of the "ship that couldn't sink" . . . and the stark reality that life does not always bend to accommodate our plans and ambitions.

On entering the exhibit, each participant received a "boarding card" that contained an actual passenger's name along with background information about the individual. At the very end of the exhibit, participants could compare the name on the card with a list of those who survived the *Titanic*, and with a list of those who did not. It was sobering to see the lists, and to realize that most of those who sailed on the ship—two of every three—did not survive.[2]

Across the corridor from the lists of victims and survivors were a half-dozen stories of individuals aboard the *Titanic* who had some connection to the city of Chicago. Having stopped to read most of the exhibits, I nearly passed by this last section; then I happened to see the words "Moody Church." I immediately stopped and began reading the tragic, triumphant story of the Reverend John Harper.

Rev. Harper was traveling to America aboard the *Titanic* to minister at the Moody Memorial Church in Chicago. His wife had died a few years earlier, so his six-year-old daughter, Nana, and her nanny, Miss Leitch, accompanied him on the journey. When the ship began sinking, Harper placed his daughter and her nanny into a lifeboat, and they were spared. He, however, was not.

When Moody Memorial Church heard the news of the *Titanic*'s sinking, they sent a delegation to New York City to see what they could do to help the daughter and her nanny. Because the young girl was left with little in the way of financial resources, the church took up a collection to help with her education.

The story fascinated me, and I wanted to know more about Rev. Harper. One persistent story reported that he survived the initial moment when the *Titanic* slipped beneath the ocean. Plunged into the water with many others, he was heard swimming about asking people if they knew the Lord. One man from Canada who survived the sinking of the *Titanic* claimed to have come to a personal relationship with Jesus Christ because of Rev. Harper's ministry in those frigid waters.

A Letter of Comfort

On May 1, 1912, the leadership of Moody Memorial Church wrote a six-page letter to the congregation of the Walworth Road Baptist Church in London, where Rev. Harper had pastored, to express their condolences. The letter, bathed in Scripture, was a moving testimony to this man who was beloved on both continents. It read, in part:

> *It may be that he suggested to that Orchestra to play "Nearer My God to Thee" in the last moments. Surely that was his thought and prayer and faith. As he stood on the deck, the night before in the after glow and looked at the red in the Western sky, he said, "It will be beautiful in the morning." How true that prophecy was for him. "Though our outward man perisheth, yet the inward man is renewed day by day, for our light affliction which is but for a moment, worketh for us a far exceeding and eternal weight of glory." Therefore, we are—"willing rather to be absent from the body and to be present with the Lord."* [3]

From a human perspective one struggles to make sense of the tragic sinking of the *Titanic* and its horrible loss of life. Why did so many perish, including this wonderful man of God? The leadership of Moody Church did not presume to know or understand. But they instinctively knew where to go when life's harder questions defied easy answers. Second Corinthians 4:16–17 and 5:8 (KJV), the two Scripture passages quoted above in their letter, reminded them that God's plans extend beyond this life to include a life everlasting that cannot be marred by personal tragedy. God's Word gave them an eternal perspective, and this eternal perspective gave them comfort and hope.

Jerusalem's Sad Objection

The exiles from Jerusalem also struggled to make sense of their terrible tragedy. They had been ripped from their homes, robbed of all their wealth, denied access to the city where their beloved temple once stood, deprived of the basic freedoms they had taken for granted, and forced to work for others in a foreign land. And yet here was the prophet Isaiah announcing God's comfort! How could such a promise ever be for them? Their pitiful circumstances caused them to doubt, and their skepticism reached a climax when the "voice" from the wilderness encouraged them to "cry out" to others in joyful anticipation of the Lord's soon return (verse 6).

After urging the people to cry out, Isaiah introduces another actor in this divine drama. The new individual is identified simply as "he" or "I," depending on the translation. He begins speaking in the second line of verse 6. Most likely Isaiah intends this to be a personification of Jerusalem. That is, Isaiah has the city of Jerusalem speak on behalf of all its citizens who have been torn from its midst.

Jerusalem offers a realistic rejoinder to the prophet. "What shall I cry?" the city shouts back (verse 6). It's as if the city looks at the prophet, puts its hands on its hips, rolls its eyes, and says, "Are you insane! Look at me! What possible reason for hope could I have?"

If the world is divided into optimists and pessimists—those who believe the glass is half full and those who believe it is half empty—Jerusalem has concluded that the glass is completely empty . . . and lies shattered on the floor!

In Isaiah 40:4, the prophet offered hope by using imagery taken from the Judean wilderness. Not to be outdone, the city skeptically responds with images from the same wilderness. "All men are like grass, and all their glory is like the flowers of the field. The grass withers and the flowers fall, because the breath of the LORD blows on them" (verses 6b–7a).

Israel's year divides into two seasons—the rainy season and the dry season. The rainy season usually begins in October and can extend into April. During these months, a reasonable amount of precipitation falls in the hills of Judah. Far less makes it over the top of the mountains to fall as rain in the Judean wilderness. But, in a good year, up to eight inches of rain can fall in this area. And if it does, a remarkable transformation takes place.

A thin carpet of grass begins to sprout on the barren hillsides, and the white, chalky wilderness starts to turn a pale shade of green. Flowers follow, and some hills take on the red blush of poppies mixed in among the green grass. Streams of water begin flowing through the dry canyons, and one could almost believe the desert was transforming itself and coming to life.

But then the rainy season ends, and the streams in the canyons dry up. The flowers start to wilt, and the grass begins to fade. An inexperienced visitor might still hope that the rain will return to rejuvenate the grass and flowers, but those who have lived in the wilderness know better. They know that, very soon, a hot, dry wind will begin to blow off the Arabian desert. Much like someone turning on a giant hair dryer and holding it against the fragile grass and flowers, this hot blast of air blows any remaining moisture from the plants. Almost overnight they fade and wither, until their stunted brown stems become nearly invisible against the rocky hillsides. What had just a short time earlier seemed to be so alive has once again returned to a barren waste.

The voice that Isaiah gives to the city of Jerusalem shouts back at the prophet, "You want to talk about the wilderness? Well, I'm like the grass and flowers that grow in the wilderness during the winter. Once I was alive and had hope. But the hot breath of God's judgment blew against me . . . and I withered and died. Look at me now! Look at my circumstances! My buildings are burned, my people have been exiled, and my hope is gone."

Circumstances often shape our perception of reality. What is real, from our perspective, is what we can see, hear, touch, and hold in our hands. When God's Word doesn't square with what we see around us, we struggle to believe God. This is the very struggle being voiced by Jerusalem. If Isaiah 40 had ended here, we could all walk away, totally depressed. But, thank God, Isaiah answers Jerusalem's objection.

Some individuals, when faced with life's harsh realities, try to pretend that their problems don't really exist. It's as if they can make their problems go away by ignoring them. When our children were growing up, we had a wonderful dog named Ginger. Ginger was a "Heinz" dog, one of those "57-varieties" kinds. She looked like a cross between a beagle and a Labrador retriever. Ginger was great with kids, but she had one major weakness that constantly got her into trouble. Her sense of smell was just too good! She had the bad habit of sniffing out—and devouring—forbidden items like hidden Christmas candy, packages of hot dog buns, pans of brownies, and any other food left unattended.

It didn't matter if the food was sealed in plastic, placed in another room, or pushed to the back of the counter. Ginger just followed her nose and then let her imagination and creativity discover a way to snag the prize!

After we discovered the empty pan, or the chewed-up wrappers, we could usually trace the trail of evidence to the spot where Ginger was hiding. Standing in front of her, we would say in our sternest voice, "Ginger! Did you do this?" Her response was classic. She would freeze and stare off to the side, refusing to make eye contact. It's as if she thought, *If I can't see them, then they can't see me!*

Unfortunately, the ploy never worked for Ginger. And neither does it work for us. Pretending that a problem doesn't exist will not make it go away. There must be a better solution. And that is what Isaiah provides.

Isaiah responds to Jerusalem by agreeing with one key part of the city's objection. "Surely the people are grass. The grass withers and the flowers fall" (verses 7b–8a). Indeed, we are like the fragile grass that grows in the Judean wilderness. People come and go. Problems come and go. The struggles of life come and go. To pretend that we will not face problems in this life is an unrealistic response. The blasting wind of trouble will indeed blow against us. But this does *not* mean that we must become pessimists!

Isaiah turns the argument on its head by adding a bold assertion. Yes, problems do come and go in this life, "but the word of our God stands forever" (verse 8b). Circumstances are *temporary;* God's Word of promise is *eternal.* The proper response to problems and difficulties is to acknowledge their existence but to remember that they are finite. There will come a time when those problems will fade away. But the promises given to us by God in His Word will last throughout our life and on into eternity. And knowing this fact can give us great comfort.

God's Words of Promise

Perspective matters. The people saw in their circumstances the hot breath of God's judgment. Isaiah looked beyond those circumstances and saw instead the rock-solid message of hope spoken by God in His Word. The people felt only a capricious wind that brought heartache and trouble. He heard God's solemn word of promise that could survive any assault. They looked for the "breath of the LORD" in their pitiful condition. He focused on the "word of our God" in the Bible. Both sought a message from God, but only Isaiah found the one that brings comfort.

And that same message of comfort and hope is available to you . . . if you follow the same path chosen by Isaiah.

Are you struggling with loneliness and rejection? God's Word of promise that stands forever is this: "Never will I leave you; never will I forsake you" (Hebrews 13:5). Are you so confused about life that you don't even know what you ought to pray for? God's Word of promise is this: "We do not know what we ought to pray for, but the Spirit himself intercedes for us with groans that words cannot express. And he who searches our hearts knows the mind of the Spirit, because the Spirit intercedes for the saints in accordance with God's will" (Romans 8:26–27).

Have you been traumatized by events beyond your own control? God's Word of promise is this: "Do not be anxious about anything, but in everything, by prayer and petition, with thanksgiving, present your requests to God. And the peace of God, which transcends all understanding, will guard your hearts and your minds in Christ Jesus" (Philippians 4:6–7).

Are you facing a temptation that seems to have you in its sights? God's Word of promise is this: "No temptation has seized you except what is common to man. And God is faithful; he will not let you be tempted beyond what you can bear. But when you are tempted, he will also provide a way out so that you can stand up under it" (1 Corinthians 10:13).

Circumstances, troubles, problems, difficulties, and temptations all come and go in our lives. The timing and intensity is unique to each person, but we all will experience them. And when that time of testing comes, we must remember that no problem will last forever. That which is eternal is God . . . and His Word. So when problems pound on the door of your life, let God's Word be there to face them. Read it. Meditate over it. Memorize it. It will provide comfort when the times of struggle come.

As the mother of four children, I have spent a lot of time in the waiting room of doctors' offices. But this wait in the doctor's office was the longest wait of my life.

Just days before, my husband, Larry, and I had sat in this same office—with our hands gripped together—looking intently in the eyes of a doctor and heard those dreadful words: "You have an advanced case of breast cancer. I don't know if this will be a death sentence or not. We will have to do additional tests."

A wait of several days followed as doctors and technicians completed comprehensive tests on my entire body. Finally the day arrived to hear the report.

Our faces announced the intensity of our emotions to almost every-one in the room. One well-dressed lady sitting on the other side of the room glanced in our direction with a knowing look and a warm smile.

We have had lots of support from close friends over the years, but the ministry of that stranger was just what we needed that day. Her glance was encouraging, but she did more than give us a warm smile. She got up from her seat, came over, sat down, and gently touched both of us. I will never forget the simple words she expressed as she reached out to touch our arms. "I understand what you are feeling and thinking," she said softly.

In addition to letting us know she understood what we were feeling and thinking, she let us know that she would be praying for us. Those words from a total stranger made such a big difference in our spirits. Why? Because they reminded us of God's love and of His promise to remain with us always. "I will never desert you, nor will I ever forsake you" (Hebrews 13:5 NASB).

Annie Mercer, coauthor, A Gift from God Workbook

Chicago, Illinois

Postcards from the Wilderness

Postcards from the Wilde

Postcards from the Wilder

Postcards from the Wilderness

Chapter Four

The Comfort of God's Person

Isaiah 40:9–11

I'm a visual learner. I grasp concepts more quickly—and remember them more completely—if I can visualize them in a concrete way. I remember the outline of Isaiah 1–35 by picturing a stone being thrown into a pond. The spot where God's stone of judgment first lands is Judah (Isaiah 1–12). God announces His judgment against Judah, and the judgment will not end until the coming of the Messiah. But when a stone is thrown into a pond, ripples immediately begin radiating out from the point of impact. Those first ripples help me visualize Isaiah 13–23. In these chapters, God turns from Judah to the surrounding nations and says to them, "If I'm going to judge Judah, what makes you think you will escape?"

Eventually the ripples travel all the way to the edge of the pond. And those ripples that lap against the shore remind me of Isaiah 24–35. In these chapters, God announces that His wrath will eventually reach all the earth. The world will experience God's judgment until the Messiah returns to establish His kingdom.

Visualizing a Truth

A truth that is visualized is a truth that can be remembered!

One way we visualize important events in our lives is by taking photographs. These visual reminders capture a slice of time and preserve it. Years after a photograph is taken, we can look at it and experience a flood of memories and emotions—all triggered by that one image. It can be a special vacation . . . or a favorite relative who has since passed away. Sometimes it can be nothing more than a snapshot of a group of childhood friends enjoying some simple pleasure long forgotten in our rapid-paced lives. But when we look at the picture, the memories pour back in an instant; it's as if the event happened just yesterday.

Isaiah shouts to the messenger bringing God's good news to "go up on a high mountain" and "lift up your voice with a shout." The word of comfort to be shouted to Jerusalem and all the towns of Judah is one of joyful expectancy: "Here is your God!" (verse 9). But who exactly is this God who is promising to come to their aid? Isaiah reaches into his tunic and pulls out two photographs of this great God to share with the people. Let's look carefully at each picture.

The first picture of God appears in verse 10. The picture is strong and striking, full of action. This bold portrait reveals a God of might and power and justice. "See, the Sovereign LORD comes with power, and his arm rules for him. See, his reward is with him, and his recompense accompanies him."

The image we see is that of God displaying the power and might of a conquering hero. But how does this picture help us gain comfort?

When we are discouraged and downhearted, it's often because our problems seem far too big for us to handle. They tower over us like mountains reaching to the heavens. We feel so small and weak standing before these giants that we can't even begin to imagine how they can be conquered. And that's when we are to pull out Isaiah's first picture of God.

Our problems may be too big for us, but they are not too big for our God. He has the ability to do anything. Well, actually He has the ability to do anything consistent with His character and attributes. After all, He can't sin. Nor can He break a promise He has made. This first picture of God shows Him as the all-powerful Lord of the universe. No problem you face is too big or too strong for Him.

In Isaiah's day this picture of God was extremely important, because the various nations played a kind of my-god-is-bigger-than-your-god game. The Babylonians claimed to have taken Jerusalem because the gods of Babylon had been stronger than the God of Judah. One reason God announced the Babylonian captivity more than a century before it happened was so that the people of Judah would understand His power and might. They went into captivity because He had announced it in advance. In fact, they went into captivity in Babylon *because* He ordered it as His judgment on the sins of His people, not because the gods of Babylon had been too strong for Him to fight off.

The people of Judah needed to be reminded that their God is a God of great strength and power. But this might not be as big a problem for you. It is very possible that you believe God is big enough to handle any problem that could come into your life . . . if He wanted to. But you might be discouraged because you doubt that God cares enough for you to want to help you in your time of need. That is, you might feel that your problems have *nothing* to do with His inability to help, but that they have *everything* to do with His unwillingness to help. He could solve your problems if He wanted to, but He just doesn't care enough about you to get involved. And if you struggle with those feelings, Isaiah wants you to look carefully at his second photograph.

Photograph #2: A Portrait of God's Compassion

As Isaiah reaches out to show us his second picture of God, we immediately notice several differences between this picture and the first one. The background in this picture is pastoral, not military. We see a tender shepherd, not a mighty warrior. The colors are warm and inviting, and we are immediately drawn to this photograph. This picture is also of God, but it shows Him as a tender shepherd.

The Judean wilderness is the home of the shepherd. This is where David tended his father's flocks. So it seems appropriate to picture God as a shepherd. But Isaiah does not picture God as some underling who cares little for the sheep in his care. No, God is the Great Shepherd who gently leads and feeds His flock. "He tends his flock like a shepherd: He gathers the lambs in his arms and carries them close to his heart; he gently leads those that have young" (verse 11).

God may have the power to do anything He wants, but this picture of God clearly shows what God wants to do most. He wants to hold His lambs in His arms and gently lead those who so desperately need His help. He is the compassionate Shepherd. If you are struggling today with a problem, do not continue reading until you can clearly see this picture. The God of the universe can do *anything*, but the one thing He most wants to do is to gently lift you up in His arms and hold you close to His heart. He loves you. He wants to care for you. He wants to meet your every need! He wants to give you the comfort that only He can supply. Don't ever let this picture slip from your memory!

A short time ago my wife and I had the privilege of spending a weekend in Sebring, Florida, where I was speaking at a church conference. A friend from the church let us stay in her guest cottage on Lake Jackson. While the temperature plummeted in Chicago, we sat on the cottage porch watching ducks floating serenely beside the dock as a lone crane waded through the water just offshore. It was a welcome respite in an otherwise hectic schedule.

As the pastor and his wife drove us around Sebring, they asked if we would like to see the house where Charles Weigle composed the great hymn "No One Ever Cared for Me Like Jesus." I knew and loved the song, but I didn't know the story behind it, so the pastor shared some of the details.

(When I got back to Chicago I searched out more of the poignant story behind Weigle and his writing of that song.)

Charles Weigle was an itinerant evangelist and songwriter who experienced a long, dark period of great personal despair when his wife walked away from their marriage. For a time he was so lonely and despondent that he even contemplated suicide. During this time Weigle was invited to Sebring, Florida, by George Sebring, the Christian developer who founded the town. Sebring reached out to help his friend regain his spiritual and emotional bearings.

A Musical Tribute to God's Compassion

The time Weigle spent on Lake Jackson was a time of personal renewal. One morning he thought about his life and muttered to himself, "No one ever cared for me like Jesus." The thought overwhelmed him. With the inspiration borne from that wonderful truth, he went to the piano to put his thoughts to music. The song he wrote remains his tribute to God's compassion during that dark period in his life.

Arriving back at the cottage where we were staying, I walked to the porch and gazed out over that beautiful lake. And in that quiet moment I thought about the truth Weigle discovered for himself while staring over these same placid waters. He encountered God's boundless love and compassion in a time of deep need and found that heaven's Eternal Shepherd continues to offer His comfort and care to all in need. Indeed, no one does care for us like Jesus!

No One Ever Cared for Me Like Jesus

I would love to tell you what I think of Jesus
Since I found in Him a friend so strong and true;
I would tell you how He changed my life completely—
He did something that no other friend could do.

All my life was full of sin when Jesus found me,
All my heart was full of misery and woe;
Jesus placed His strong and loving arms about me,
And He led me in the way I ought to go.

Ev'ry day He comes to me with new assurance,
More and more I understand His words of love;
But I'll never know just why He came to save me,
Till some day I see His blessed face above.

Refrain

No one ever cared for me like Jesus,
There's no other friend so kind as He;
No one else could take the sin and darkness from me—
O how much He cared for me! [1]

Several years ago a serious car accident left my daughter Barb unconscious with severe head injuries. Anxiety gripped my wife, Dottie, and me during Barb's two lengthy brain surgeries. We felt utterly helpless as we faced her possible death or permanent brain damage.

Our frustration intensified as our then-seventeen-year-old daughter continued unconscious for ten weeks—and underwent sixteen surgeries during her half-a-year stay in the hospital.

And yet Barb improved—though ever so gradually—to the amazement of her many doctors, nurses, and therapists. In the long hours of waiting and of desperation, we also experienced God's peace. As we placed her in God's hands to do as He sovereignly desired, we were assured that "His way is blameless" (Psalm 18:30 NASB), regardless of the outcome.

Barb fully recovered and today is married and has three children. She is grateful to the Lord for His marvelous working in her life. She, our son, and my wife and I are also deeply grateful to the many friends who rallied to our needs, giving lovingly and unsparingly of their time and energy.

I will never forget the immense comfort Dottie and I experienced when several friends stayed with us at the hospital during several of Barb's surgeries. Their presence vividly communicated the message, "We care, and we want to carry the burden with you."

During Barb's months of recovery, several friends volunteered to sit with her in the hospital for hours at a time each week. Others brought meals to our home.

Cards with handwritten notes and phone calls were especially uplifting. One friend mailed to Dottie a three-by-five card with the verse, "I will take refuge in the shadow of your wings until the disaster is passed" (Psalm. 57:1b). Dottie clung to that promise with great hope.

We thank the Lord for His comfort, ministered to us by loving friends.

Roy B. Zuck, senior professor emeritus of Bible exposition
Dallas Theological Seminary, Dallas, Texas

Postcards from the Wilderness

The image of God as a shepherd is an enduring favorite throughout the Bible. David pictured the Lord as his Shepherd in Psalm 23. "The LORD is my shepherd, I shall not be in want" (23:1). And Jesus described Himself as the Good Shepherd in John 10. "I am the good shepherd. The good shepherd lays down his life for the sheep" (10:11).

Just before describing Himself as the Good Shepherd, Jesus announced that He had come to earth to help restore humanity's relationship to God—to serve as the bridge between us and our heavenly Father. Jesus said, "I have come that they may have life, and have it to the full" (John 10:10b). God's ultimate desire for us is to have eternal life—which is life in the fullest sense both now and in eternity.

Jesus came to earth to provide eternal life, but a quick look at the world tells us that something must be horribly wrong. Hatred, evil, greed, sorrow, suffering, and pain seem to crowd out the life promised by God. If God had such wonderful plans for His creation, why do we struggle so?

The Bible provides the answer, and it says that our key problem is sin. "For all have sinned and fall short of the glory of God" (Romans 3:23). We have deliberately chosen to violate God's standards of right and wrong, and the Bible calls this sin. Sin has carved a deep chasm between us and the Lord, and the gulf is too great to be spanned by us alone.

God's justice demands that those guilty of a crime pay the penalty. We have violated God's standards of right and wrong, and the penalty for that violation is eternal death—a separation from God both now and forever. "For the wages of sin is death" (Romans 6:23a).

God's justice demands payment for sin, but God's love sought to find a way to bridge the gap between Him and us. And the solution came through the life, death, and resurrection of His Son, Jesus Christ. Here the Good Shepherd would lay down His life. Jesus loved you so much that He willingly came to earth, lived a perfect life, and then died on the cross. Why? To pay the penalty for your sins and mine. But unlike any other shepherd, the Good Shepherd rose from the dead. By rising from the grave, He demonstrated that His death was sufficient to pay the price.

Jesus has provided the one and only way that we can cross over the chasm from death and despair to eternal life. He Himself said, "I am the way and the truth and the life. No one comes to the Father except through me" (John 14:6).

The Good Shepherd Who Gave His Life . . . for You

Have you ever made a personal decision to place your trust for eternal life in Him? Do you believe that when Jesus died on the cross, He died to pay the penalty for your sins? Are you willing to trust Him for your eternal destiny—to place your life in His hands? Are you willing to accept Him as your Good Shepherd whom you can follow in this life—and for eternity? If you are, you can do so right now by praying a simple prayer like the following:

Dear Lord, I know that my life is empty without You. I believe You love me so much that You sent Your Son, Jesus Christ, to die on the cross to pay the penalty for my sin. I now want to place my trust in Jesus Christ

as the substitute for my sin. Please forgive me of my sin
and give me eternal life. In Christ's name I ask this.
Amen.

Did you just pray this prayer? If so, read Isaiah 40:11 again and embrace the truth that "he gathers the lambs in his arms and carries them close to his heart." You are now one of God's lambs, and His desire is to carry you near His heart. Will all your problems disappear? No, they won't. But you can walk through life knowing that you are not facing your problems alone.

Whether you just placed your faith in Jesus Christ or whether you made this great decision years ago, the truth you must remember from Isaiah 40:11 is that the God of the universe, the Great Shepherd, will watch over you and gently carry you along through life. How can you be sure? Remember this: If God loved you so much that He sent His only Son to die on the cross so you could have your sins forgiven and receive eternal life, then He also loves you enough to care for the smaller day-to-day burdens you face in your life. Count on it!

Many years ago, after a long journey of self-absorption and self-destruction, I finally turned to Jesus Christ for a personal relationship and became a Christian. My spirit was instantly made alive, but my mind, will, and emotions still needed to be conformed to Christ's image (Romans 8:29).

That's when I quit drinking, though I secretly resented the restriction of my "right" to personal pleasure. That resulted in a self-righteous and judgmental attitude toward others. Six years later my husband and our family moved away from loving Christian friends. Sadly, I started drinking again to escape the pain of loneliness and misunderstanding. Chaos prevailed in my life, even though I attended church and served in a number of ministries.

Two Christian friends kept praying long-distance for me at this time of spiritual desolation. They claimed for me Psalm 107:20: "He sent His word and healed them, and delivered them from their destructions" (NASB). Finally, I "hit bottom." Recognizing my impossible struggle with alcohol, I cried out to the Lord Jesus that I couldn't go on living lies. I needed Him! Calling drunkenness by its real name—sin—I confessed it to God, asking Him to show me His glory, love, and mercy. Jesus Christ immediately met me there!

I began to see God's glory and majesty and also to understand the depravity of my own sinful nature. For days I wept with new awareness of who God is in Christ. But now they were

Postcards from the Wilderness

tears of repentance and joy. I asked Him to deliver me from my addiction and sin.

I know now I am "a new creature" in Christ; "the old things passed away; behold, new things have come" (2 Corinthians 5:17 NASB). Understanding His love for me—and growing in my love for Him—allowed me the freedom to let His love cast out my fear of drinking (1 John 4:18). By His grace and power, I have experienced full deliverance from even a desire for alcohol (John 8:32, 36).

Nancy Norvell Smitz, chairman, First Ladies' Prayer Brunch of Tampa Bay; wife, Tampa, Florida

Postcards from the Wilde

Postcards from the Wilderness

Chapter Five

The Comfort of God's Protection

Isaiah 40:12–26

In the Poets' Corner of Westminster Abbey, just to the left of the bust of Alfred Tennyson, hangs a plaque dedicated to the memory of Granville Sharp. Sharp was a literary and biblical scholar who is best known in scholarly circles for the "Granville Sharp Rule," an obscure but important rule in Greek grammar.

Because of his contribution to the understanding of language, the location of Sharp's memorial among England's literary giants is entirely in order. But what is amazing is that the plaque says nothing about Sharp's literary achievements. The thing for which Sharp is memorialized is far more significant. And, as commentator Paul Harvey would say, here is "the rest of the story."

Granville Sharp was born in Durham, England, in 1735. His father was an archdeacon in the Church of England, and his grandfather was the archbishop of York. Yet in spite of these strong family ties to the ministry, Sharp decided against a career in the Church of England. Instead, he moved to London, where he eventually become a clerk in the civil service.

In many ways he lived an unassuming, modest life. He devoted his extra time to his literary pursuits, and this could have been the sum of his career—had he not met Jonathan Strong.

A Beaten Slave

In 1765 Sharp was living with his brother, a surgeon, in East London when Strong arrived at the door seeking medical help. Strong was a black slave who had been so badly beaten by his master that he was close to death. Moved by compassion, Granville Sharp took Strong to a nearby hospital, where Strong spent four months recovering from his injuries.

While Strong recuperated in the hospital, Sharp would visit him regularly. During those visits Strong told Sharp how his master had brought him to England from Barbados, been dissatisfied with his services, beaten him, and eventually thrown him out into the street as one might throw away a worn-out coat.

After Strong had regained his health, his master paid some men to recapture him because he realized this "property" might again have some value. When Granville Sharp heard the news, he took the slave master to court, claiming that because Strong was in England he was no longer a slave. In 1768 the courts ruled in Strong's favor. Energized by this victory, Granville took up the cases of other slaves and convinced the courts that "as soon as any slave sets foot upon English territory, he becomes free."

Freeing the Slaves

Another slave helped by Granville was a man named James Somerset. Sharp put Somerset in contact with Francis Hargrave, a young lawyer who shared Sharp's hatred of slavery. In 1772 the courts ruled that Somerset should go free because slavery was "so odious, that nothing can be suffered to support it." This ruling effectively brought about freedom for the slaves of England, Ireland, and Wales. A similar ruling in 1778—again engineered by Sharp—freed those slaves residing in Scotland. Slavery in England was gone, but the slave trade still remained . . . so Sharp pressed on.

In 1787 Sharp and several friends formed the Society for the Abolition of the Slave Trade. They persuaded William Wilberforce, a member of Parliament, to be their spokesman in the House of Commons. Wilberforce is often hailed as the man who helped abolish the slave trade throughout the British Empire, but few know of Granville Sharp's tireless efforts in this noble endeavor.

The plaque in the Poets' Corner at Westminster Abbey hints at his achievements (see page 64). The top of the memorial has a picture of Granville Sharp. To his left is an African slave in chains with his right knee bowed in prayer. To his right a lion and a lamb stand together, imagery from Isaiah 11 that promises a time of peace God will someday bring to this world.

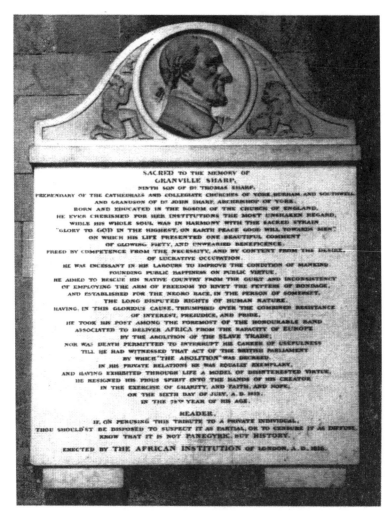

SACRED TO THE MEMORY OF
GRANVILLE SHARP,
NINTH SON OF Dr THOMAS SHARP,
PREBENDARY OF THE CATHEDRALS AND COLLEGIATE CHURCHES OF YORK, DURHAM, AND SOUTHWELL,
AND GRANDSON OF Dr JOHN SHARP, ARCHBISHOP OF YORK.
BORN AND EDUCATED IN THE BOSOM OF THE CHURCH OF ENGLAND,
HE EVER CHERISHED FOR HER INSTITUTIONS THE MOST UNSHAKEN REGARD,
WHILE HIS WHOLE SOUL WAS IN HARMONY WITH THE SACRED STRAIN
"GLORY TO GOD IN THE HIGHEST, ON EARTH PEACE GOOD WILL TOWARDS MEN":
ON WHICH HIS LIFE PRESENTED ONE BEAUTIFUL COMMENT
OF GLOWING PIETY, AND UNWEARIED BENEFICENCE.
FREED BY COMPETENCE FROM THE NECESSITY, AND BY CONTENT FROM THE DESIRE,
OF LUCRATIVE OCCUPATION,
HE WAS INCESSANT IN HIS LABOURS TO IMPROVE THE CONDITION OF MANKIND
FOUNDING PUBLIC HAPPINESS ON PUBLIC VIRTUE.
HE AIMED TO RESCUE HIS NATIVE COUNTRY FROM THE GUILT AND INCONSISTENCY
OF EMPLOYING THE ARM OF FREEDOM TO RIVET THE FETTERS OF BONDAGE,
AND ESTABLISHED FOR THE NEGRO RACE, IN THE PERSON OF SOMERSET,
THE LONG DISPUTED RIGHTS OF HUMAN NATURE.
HAVING, IN THIS GLORIOUS CAUSE, TRIUMPHED OVER THE COMBINED RESISTANCE
OF INTEREST, PREJUDICE, AND PRIDE,
HE TOOK HIS POST AMONG THE FOREMOST OF THE HONOURABLE BAND
ASSOCIATED TO DELIVER AFRICA FROM THE RAPACITY OF EUROPE
BY THE ABOLITION OF THE SLAVE TRADE;
NOR WAS DEATH PERMITTED TO INTERRUPT HIS CAREER OF USEFULNESS
TILL HE HAD WITNESSED THAT ACT OF THE BRITISH PARLIAMENT
BY WHICH "THE ABOLITION" WAS DECREED.
IN HIS PRIVATE RELATIONS HE WAS EQUALLY EXEMPLARY,
AND HAVING EXHIBITED THROUGH LIFE A MODEL OF DISINTERESTED VIRTUE,
HE RESIGNED HIS PIOUS SPIRIT INTO THE HANDS OF HIS CREATOR
IN THE EXERCISE OF CHARITY, AND FAITH, AND HOPE,
ON THE SIXTH DAY OF JULY, A.D. 1813,
IN THE 78TH YEAR OF HIS AGE.

READER,
IF, ON PERUSING THIS TRIBUTE TO A PRIVATE INDIVIDUAL,
THOU SHOULD'ST BE DISPOSED TO SUSPECT IT AS PARTIAL, OR TO CENSURE IT AS DIFFUSE,
KNOW THAT IT IS NOT PANEGYRIC, BUT HISTORY.

ERECTED BY THE AFRICAN INSTITUTION OF LONDON, A.D. 1816.

Below these images are the words that forever memorialize Granville Sharp, the literary giant who did much for Greek grammar—but who did so much more for humanity. The plaque reads, in part, as follows:

Sacred to the memory of Granville Sharp, . . .
born and educated in the bosom of the Church of England,
he ever cherished for her institutions the most unshaken regard,
while his whole soul was in harmony with the sacred strain
"Glory to God in the highest, on earth peace good will towards men,"
on which his life presented one beautiful comment
of glowing piety, and unwearied beneficence. . . .
[H]e aimed to rescue his native country from the guilt
and inconsistency
of employing the arm of freedom to rivet the fetters of bondage,
and established for the negro race, in the person of Somerset,
the long disputed rights of human nature.
Having, in this glorious cause, triumphed over
the combined resistance
of interest, prejudice and pride,
he took his post among the foremost of the honourable band
associated to deliver Africa from the rapacity of Europe
by the abolition of the slave trade; . . .
In his private relations he was equally exemplary,
and having exhibited through life a model of disinterested virtue,
he resigned his pious spirit into the hands of his Creator
in the exercise of charity, and faith, and hope,
on the sixth day of July, A.D. 1813
in the 78th year of his age. . . .
Erected by The African Institution of London, A.D. 1816

What turned a mild-mannered civil servant into a fear-
less activist who boldly stood against evil and "triumphed
over the combined resistance of interest, prejudice and
pride"? The key was his relationship to God: "His whole soul

was in harmony with the sacred strain, 'Glory to God in the highest, on earth peace good will towards men.' " Granville Sharp understood the nature and character of God, and he sought to make God's life a reality in his own, such that "his life presented one beautiful comment of glowing piety, and unwearied beneficence."

But how does the life of Granville Sharp relate to the exiles from Judah who were living in Babylon? Like those in exile who were reading the words of the prophet Isaiah, Sharp faced problems and difficulties that seemed insurmountable. He sought to change the entire social fabric of the British Empire. In doing so, he found himself opposed by powerful people who had made their fortunes through the slave trade, and who stood to lose much if it was abolished. In a similar fashion, the exiles from Judah found themselves facing the might of the Babylonian Empire. The nation of Babylon, the idols of Babylon, the king of Babylon, and the spiritual forces behind the kingdom all conspired to keep the people of Judah in slavery. Where could God's people go to find protection? Isaiah supplies the answer for them—and for us.

Promises, Promises

We can make great promises, but can we deliver on them? For example, I could promise to send you a check for one million dollars if you would just write to me and ask for it. Of course, if I made such a promise to you, I would be lying. I don't have sufficient resources in my bank account to begin to cover a small portion of even one such check. So my promise would be nothing more than empty words.

In Isaiah 40:1–11 the prophet recorded several great promises made by God. No obstacle is too big to keep God from you. Circumstances can change, but God's word of promise to you will stand forever. God is all-powerful and He can do anything, yet the thing He most wants to do is to hold you in His arms: "He gathers the lambs in his arms and carries them" (verse 11). Those are powerful words of hope and comfort, but they are only valid if the One making them can keep His word.

So how much can we depend on the God who is making these promises? Can He deliver?

Isaiah helps us focus on the reality of God's promised protection by asking and answering four sets of questions. Each set of questions is designed to make us think first about God's true nature and character. Then Isaiah applies this truth about God to the different problems we face in life. His goals are to help us gain a greater understanding of God and to help us realize how much our God can protect us against all the troubles we face in life.

Comparing Nations to God (verses 12–17)

As a teacher, I envision verses 12–14 as Isaiah's "pop quiz" to his audience. I can almost hear him say, "Class, take out a blank sheet of lined notebook paper and put your name at the top." Are you prepared to take Isaiah's quiz? Here are the questions, updated for today. They divide into two separate groups. The first group of questions is in verse 12.

1. Who can hold all the water of the world in the hollow of His hand?

2. Who can measure the distance from one end of the universe to the other?

3. Who can calculate the mass of all the mountains in the world?

So far you probably are doing okay on the quiz. The answer to each of the first three questions is *God*. He alone knows all these details about the universe because He is the One who created it. But in the second group of questions, in verses 13–14, Isaiah changes his focus.

4. Who knows as much as God?

5. Where did God go to school to become so wise?

6. Who taught God all His knowledge about the universe?

These questions were a little more difficult, but I'm confident you still got the answers right. No one knows as much as God, and He did not consult with anyone to gain all His knowledge. He is the only one who knows all things because He alone is the one who fashioned the universe.

But what is the point of these questions? Why does Isaiah ask questions with such obvious answers? He does so to remind us what the God of the universe is really like. The God who promises to hold us in His arms, close to His heart, is the God who understands everything in the universe. Indeed, He is the God who created the entire universe. Now, compared to a God like that, how significant are your troubles?

The major problem faced by the exiles of Judah was the Babylonian Empire that had enslaved them. This is the nation that had conquered the kingdom of Judah, destroyed the city of Jerusalem, captured and exiled the people, and burned down their temple to God. The Babylonian Empire had certainly proven itself to be stronger than the people of

Judah. But how strong was this empire compared to the God of the universe? Having asked a series of questions to get us thinking about God, Isaiah now helps us understand how the might of the Babylonian Empire pales in comparison to such a powerful God.

Compared to God, "the nations are like a drop in a bucket; they are regarded as dust on the scales" (verse 15a). How significant is a single drop of water in a large bucket? That is how significant the greatest nation is compared to the power of the God who made the universe. In fact, giving the Babylonian Empire the importance of a single drop of water in a bucket is still more significance than it really deserves, as Isaiah continues to diminish the worth of the nations. Compared to God, the nations are as significant as

- a drop in a bucket (verse 15)
- a speck of dust on the scales (verse 15)
- nothing (verse 17), and
- less than nothing (verse 17).

What is the biggest problem you face today? Now, how big is that problem compared to the God who created the universe, who controls the universe, and who understands the inner workings of every part of the universe? Even if your problem is as big as an entire nation, it is "less than nothing" compared to the awesome power of God. You can trust His promise to protect you from such opposition.

Early in 1995, after six months of medical tests, doctors at hospitals in Dallas and Washington, D.C., diagnosed our oldest son with a rare condition called Cushing's disease. Within three months he underwent two dangerous surgeries with lengthy recovery periods. While those twelve months seemed long and very difficult, the resulting hormonal imbalance in Mark's body took our family through five additional years of struggle we had not anticipated.

Many people prayed for Mark before, during, and after his surgery. We thought God would take us through this difficult time and then allow our family to return to "normal." But the weeks turned into months and the months into years. Mark's emotional struggles affected each member of our family. He eventually dropped out of school and had no sense of purpose for his life.

During this long, drawn-out struggle, God taught us powerful lessons about who He is and what He can do. There were days when I would open my Bible and read verses just hoping there would be some word of encouragement for me to press on. Other times, I would cry out to the Lord and ask Him to carry me through the day because I could not make it through on my own.

I was unable to "fix the problem" or put any of the pieces back in place. God had orchestrated this unusual circumstance, and I realized my need to wait, rest, and seek His comfort each day. During this time, I found myself bowing before the Lord and submitting my desires to His will. I had to depend on God for any solution in Mark's life and to heal the relationships within our family.

Looking back now, I believe God wanted us to learn to trust Him for the long haul and draw upon His comfort and strength one day at a time.

Brenda McCord, staff, Moody Bible Institute; mother
Chicago, Illinois

Postcards from the Wilderness

Comparing Idols to God (verses 18–20)

Years ago Art Linkletter had a television program where he would interview children. On one show he had the children draw pictures and explain what they were making. When Mr. Linkletter asked one child what he was drawing, the child proudly answered, "God!"

Somewhat taken aback, Mr. Linkletter responded, "But, son, nobody knows what God looks like."

"They will when I get through!" responded the young child.

Years before Art Linkletter, the prophet Isaiah asked a similar set of questions to the people of Judah. "To whom, then, will you compare God? What image will you compare him to?" (verse 18). Simply put, Isaiah's challenge to the people is this: Draw God!

I'm sure they responded, "We can't! The God of the universe can't be reduced to a created, visible image. The Creator cannot be confined to a single inanimate object in time and space."

"Very good!" Isaiah must have responded. "Now that you understand this truth about the God of the universe, compare the idols of the nations to your God."

The Babylonians claimed that their gods had overpowered the God of Israel. Isaiah responded by asking the people of Judah to compare the "gods" of Babylon to the God of the universe. The true God cannot be confined to a single object, but the "gods" of Babylon were nothing more than inanimate objects fashioned by human craftsmen.

Isaiah's unmasking of Babylon's idols rivals any episode of daytime "talk television" for its comic sarcasm and in-your-face reality. Idols are nothing more than objects cast by craftsmen and overlaid by goldsmiths (verse 19). But not everyone can afford such high-class idols. "A man too poor to present such an offering selects wood that will not rot" (verse 20a). It makes one wonder if idols came with a rot-protection warranty—a guarantee from the artist for "five years or fifty thousand prayers, whichever comes first." And you certainly wanted the best craftsman working on your god so you could "set up an idol that will not topple" (verse 20b). It's just too embarrassing to have your god falling over every time you slam the door!

Isaiah might be using humor and sarcasm, but don't miss his point. The problems you face might have their roots in deep spiritual opposition. Those opposing you claim to have spiritual forces on their side that they hope will keep you cowering in fear. Isaiah asks you to take a dispassionate look at all rival "gods" and to compare them to the true God of the Bible. Compared to Him, all other spiritual foes are nothing. Your God will protect you against all false spiritual opposition.

Comparing Kings to God (verses 21–24)

Empires can be nothing more than faceless entities. To gain the support of the people, nations must often be personified in a single leader who represents the power of the empire in a visible way. In our country the power of the government is often personified in the office of the president of the United States. Though, in reality, his power is limited, he does represent in a tangible way everything that symbolizes the strength of our nation.

This has always been true in history. During the time of the Babylonian captivity, the power of the Babylonian

Empire was localized in King Nebuchadnezzar. In Daniel 2 it is Nebuchadnezzar who was the "head of gold" that was intended to symbolize the first of four successive world empires. The Jewish people feared not just the Babylonian Empire in general; they feared its leader, Nebuchadnezzar—the one who personified that empire.

Isaiah began his third set of questions by rhetorically asking the people, "Do you not know? Have you not heard? Has it not been told you from the beginning? Have you not understood since the earth was founded?" (verse 21). These questions focus on the fact that one key truth has been obvious since the beginning of creation. That truth is God's sovereign control over all the earth. "He sits enthroned above the circle of the earth, and its people are like grasshoppers" (verse 22a). God, and God alone, rules over the earth.

To the Jewish captives in Babylon, it seemed as if King Nebuchadnezzar had the power of life and death. He was the one who could sentence someone to be thrown alive into a fiery furnace. But the reality is that only the King of Kings and Lord of Lords holds such power. "He brings princes to naught and reduces the rulers of this world to nothing. No sooner are they planted, no sooner are they sown, no sooner do they take root in the ground, than he blows on them and they wither, and a whirlwind sweeps them away like chaff" (verses 23–24). Certainly these words must have come to mind to the Jewish exiles when, in a single evening, they watched God destroy King Belshazzar and hand the entire kingdom of Babylon over to the Medes and the Persians (Daniel 5).

Can you trace your current troubles to a single individual who is seeking to harm you? You have tried befriending this person, you have tried appeasing this person, you have tried confronting this person, but nothing seems to work. And now you struggle to sleep at night because you find yourself replaying the painful encounters of the previous day. What can you do?

First, you can remember that God is in control. He has the ability to take care of this problem, and He will—in His time. Second, you can take your concerns and hurts to Him in prayer. Give the matter over to God and let Him handle it. Third, having released God to handle the parts that belong to Him, you can assume control over those matters that He has given to you. And what are they? According to 1 Peter 2:13–25 you are responsible to:

- Submit to every authority.
- Do good.
- Live as servants of God.
- Show proper respect to everyone.
- Submit to those who rule over you with respect.
- Bear up under the pain of unjust suffering.
- Follow the example laid down by Christ by not retaliating.

How big is your God? Are you able to see Him as the sovereign Ruler of the universe? Do you believe that nothing can come into your life unless He permits it to happen? If so, then please remember He is in control even when you experience personal suffering, heartache, and pain at the hands of evil men and women. Until you reach eternity you may never know why He has permitted individuals or events into your life that have caused you such pain.

These are the dark times when our view of heaven is clouded and obscured. But even in the dark times we must "trust and obey," remembering the example set for us by God's own Son. "When they hurled their insults at him, he did not retaliate; when he suffered, he made no threats. Instead, he entrusted himself to him who judges justly" (1 Peter 2:23). Our God is greater than any evil that might arise against you; seek His protection.

Comparing Spiritual Forces to God (verses 25–26)

Don't fear nations. Don't fear idols. Don't fear individuals. Three good reminders from Isaiah. But the prophet has a fourth set of questions. And they are very similar to his second set of questions.

"To whom will you compare me? Or who is my equal?" (verse 25). Who is like the God who created the universe? Who comes close to matching His omnipotence, omniscience, or omnipresence? The first time he asked these questions, Isaiah compared God with idols. But in this section Isaiah focuses on the spiritual forces behind those idols.

The actual physical representation of a god or goddess might itself be nothing, but are there not spiritual forces behind those representations? The Babylonians looked to the heavens and saw astrological forces that they believed influenced the destiny of the human race. Much of what they believed is still practiced in the present day through the use of astrology and horoscopes. The ultimate question pondered by the people in Isaiah's day was this: Are there not spiritual forces in the heavens that can exert at least some control over our destiny?

Isaiah's answer is direct and forceful. "Lift your eyes and look to the heavens: Who created all these? He who brings out the starry host one by one, and calls them each by name. Because of his great power and mighty strength, not one of them is missing" (verse 26). The Babylonians worshiped the stars of the heavens. Isaiah reminds us that we worship the God who made—and who controls—the stars of the heavens! Those who allow the stars to govern their destiny are living in fear of inanimate objects. We worship the God who created all the heavenly bodies.

God's protection for us extends beyond what we can see to include the spiritual forces that do, indeed, exist in the universe. Others may live in fear of spirit beings, but we know that angels—including those fallen angels who followed Satan in his rebellion against God—are finite, created beings. They exist not because of their great power but because of God's gracious permission as part of His larger plan for His creation. But even these angelic hosts are subject to the sovereign God.

The Preeminence of Jesus Christ

Nearly eight hundred years after Isaiah penned this chapter, the apostle Paul described the humble obedience of Jesus Christ and used Him as a model to demonstrate how we ought to live. The Son of God submitted to the Father's plan of redemption, following in obedience "to death—even death on a cross" (Philippians 2:8). Then, at the proper time, God exalted Jesus to His rightful role as Messiah and Lord. Our assignment is to develop the same attitude of trusting obedience in the Father that was demonstrated by Jesus Christ. And one way to do that is to remember that the God who promises to walk with us through the troubles of life is greater than any problem we might face.

Paul's words in Philippians 2 serve as a fitting conclusion to this section of Isaiah's message because they remind us that, in the end, God does reward those who trust Him. And the example we can look to as we face life's problems is that of Jesus Christ. He "humbled himself and became obedient to death—even death on a cross! Therefore God exalted him to the highest place and gave him the name that is above every name, that at the name of Jesus every knee should bow, in heaven and on earth and under the earth, and every tongue confess that Jesus Christ is Lord, to the glory of God the Father" (Philippians 2:8–11).

Two weeks after my husband flew to Europe for an extended business trip, I was diagnosed with invasive breast cancer in my right breast. I was instructed to see a surgical oncologist and a reconstruction surgeon immediately. I called a dear Christian friend, and she burst into tears at the news of my cancer. She then insisted on going with me through the blur of doctor appointments scheduled for the next day.

The doctors did allow me to travel to Europe, but they told me I would need a mastectomy on my return. Still, I left the doctors' offices with great expectation to see how the Lord would provide for my needs as I began this wilderness journey through cancer, malignancy, and mastectomy.

As my husband and I flew from London to Turkey to join others on a Christian tour, I said to him, "I'm anxious to see whom the Lord will have on this trip to encourage me ." We only knew four of the fifty-four others on the tour. When we met with the group, I found that it included a gynecologist and a surgeon. Those two wonderful people gave me endless time to ask questions, they helped coach me on what to expect regarding the surgery, and they shared questions to ask about follow-up treatment, such as chemotherapy.

While we were traveling, our host learned of my diagnosis and imminent surgery. Toward the end of the tour, he asked if he could share this with the group. My first reaction was "No, we've all just met," but the Lord impressed on me that I should allow him to tell them.

I was not prepared for the love that flowed from my new friends. They joined all my other friends to become a legion of prayer warriors for me.

The surgery and process of recovery was physically draining, especially during the chemotherapy. But it also allowed me to experience a joy and intimacy with my beloved Savior that I didn't know was possible.

Sue Sewell, mother, wife
Dallas, Texas

Postcards from the Wilderness

Postcards from the Wilderness

Chapter Six

The Comfort of God's Power

Isaiah 40:27–31

On a wall of the basement in my house, beside the desk where I'm writing this chapter, hangs an old street sign. (No, I did not steal it!) This is not a fancy sign marking a street name; nor is it a stop sign; nor is it any other type of local, state, or federal sign. It's a street sign that pointed the way to the high school I attended, and I designed the sign years ago. But let me explain.

During my senior year at Central Columbia High School near Bloomsburg, Pennsylvania, I took a drafting class. Our school needed a new directional sign on the highway, and to provide the students in the class with some hands-on experience—and, no doubt, to save the school district some money—the instructor asked us to submit designs for the sign. My design was then selected, and it was soon etched onto a 15-by 24-inch piece of galvanized metal, glued to a thin sheet of wood, and screwed into a metal pole along the highway. The sign—white block letters on a black background—was plain but functional.

After graduation I went off to college and never returned to live in my hometown. Over time, the sign became weathered and worn. The original pole gave out, and new holes were drilled to fasten the sign to another pole. Eventually, the sign and pole collapsed. Whether they were struck by an automobile or simply fell down on their own, I don't know. But my grand sign was now nothing more than roadside junk (as you can see above).

I had completely forgotten about the sign. But a dear high school friend had not. As the sign fell into disrepair, he kept watching it. When it finally collapsed, he stopped and picked it up. And then he held onto it, waiting for an opportunity to present it to me. On a visit back to see my parents, I ran into John, and he said he had a gift for me. The gift was the old sign, weathered and bent, but still readable!

In one sense the sign had always been mine. I had designed it; I viewed it with pride when it was first installed. But in another sense it only became mine when John presented it to me. What had been mine from a distance now became mine in a personal way.

In a similar fashion, Isaiah called on the exiles of Judah to make the truth of Isaiah 40 theirs in a personal way. In the first twenty-six verses the prophet shared great truths about God's character. But beginning in verse 27, he challenged the nation to move from *information* to *application*. They now had to appropriate the truth in their own lives.

God's Power Doubted

The prophet began by challenging Israel's complaints that God didn't know—or didn't care—about their struggles. "Why do you say, O Jacob, and complain, O Israel, 'My way is hidden from the Lord; my cause is disregarded by my God'?" (verse 27). Do not mistake the silence of God for ignorance or apathy. God doesn't always answer our cries for help as quickly as we might wish, and His answer sometimes isn't the one we hoped to hear. But to demand that God follow our timetable or grant all our desires is to assume that we always know what is best.

Isaiah chastised the exiles of Judah for claiming that their struggles were "hidden" from the Lord, as if God's all-piercing eyes couldn't see the plight of His people in the land of Babylon. Even worse was their claim that God knew of their plight but simply chose to disregard it. To voice such a complaint was to misunderstand the depth of God's knowledge . . . and His love.

Have you ever doubted God's wisdom or His goodness when walking through a dark valley of despair? It's easy to do, especially if we become so focused on our struggles that we find it hard to see life from His perspective. Those are the times when we must go back to the basics: to remember that

God is a God who knows the troubles we now face and to believe that He cares deeply and intimately about our eternal well-being. One unknown poet has compared God's wise plans and our finite knowledge to the work of a weaver whose shuttle spins a tapestry the viewer cannot fully understand. The poem, "The Weaver," captures best the tension we face as we seek to reconcile our day-to-day struggles in life with our understanding and acceptance of a sovereign God who is working out His eternal plan in our lives.

The Weaver

My life is but a weaving
Between my Lord and me.
I cannot choose the colors;
He worketh steadily.

Oftimes He weaveth sorrow,
And I in foolish pride
Forget He sees the upper,
And I the underside.

Not 'til the loom is silent
And the shuttles cease to fly,
Shall God unroll the canvas
And explain the reason why.

The dark threads are as needful
In the Weaver's skillful hand,
As the threads of gold and silver
In the pattern He has planned.

Author Unknown

My teenage son Luke and I were sitting in the doctor's office when she told Luke, "Your vision is not good enough to drive." This statement hit us like a ton of bricks. Luke had lost visual clarity two years earlier when he began having migraine headaches. Two years of doctors' visits had failed to pinpoint a cause or find an effective treatment. The medical explanations were as cloudy as his vision. As we sat in the car outside the doctor's office, I held him, and we both cried.

We did not find the explanations we desired from the doctors, but the Lord faithfully brought into our lives friends who were involved with a ministry called "Twice Blessed." It is based on 2 Corinthians 1:3–4: "Blessed be the God and Father of our Lord Jesus Christ, the Father of mercies and God of all comfort, who comforts us in all our affliction so that we will be able to comfort those who are in any affliction with the comfort with which we ourselves are comforted by God" (NASB).

Through this ministry Luke has had the opportunity to express his struggles, God's comfort of joy and peace, and his faith in God's purpose during difficult days. The blurriness of his eyes has actually caused him to see and sense God in a clearer way.

Years earlier, I heard another doctor's traumatizing word. My wife's double vision was being caused by an aneurysm, a tumor, or multiple sclerosis. As a seminary student I was used to multiple-choice questions, but in this case I wanted a fourth option: none of the above. Unfortunately, further tests confirmed that Lisa had multiple sclerosis.

The MS started out slowly but eventually became all-consuming. It resulted in the loss of Lisa's ability to use her arms and legs.

Postcards from the Wilderness

Then it took the toughest one of all, her ability to see. Her day is completely at the mercy of others who help. Her bed has replaced the dinner table as the focus of conversation and interaction. It has also become the pulpit where in an unspoken way she preaches the message of grace, joy, and encouragement. The verse that she has held to during this time is Psalm 119:71: "It is good for me that I was afflicted, that I may learn Your statutes" (NASB).

I'm often asked, "How do you keep going?" The person wants to know how I cope with having a son who is legally blind, or how I'm able to care for my wife who has been bedridden for a number of years because of multiple sclerosis.

There have been times when the burdens caused me to look down and not up. I focused on the weight pressing down on my shoulders and not on the strength that He promised to supply. Yet even in those times, the Lord faithfully provided for me through His Word, His people, and His presence.

At just the right time, I always seem to receive in the mail a little brown, padded envelope from our "Wal-Mart" angel. In the envelope is a short note of encouragement and a gift card to Wal-Mart. While this may not seem like much, to me it represents a kiss of God's love and a reminder that someone cares . . . and especially that He cares.

The Lord says that He will not allow me to face more than I can bear. Putting that together with the truth that "My yoke is easy, and My load is light," I realize that it is really His load and that He promises to provide the strength to bear it. And in His faithfulness He brings along those who help remind me that He is the One who provides the strength and encouragement to keep me going.

Greg Hatteberg, director of admissions
Dallas Theological Seminary, Dallas, Texas

Postcards from the Wilderness

God's Power Explained

So what is to be our response when we face the hard times of life? Having chastised the people for their wrong response, Isaiah then shared how they ought to respond in times of discouragement and despair. He began by repeating two questions that he had asked earlier to help his readers focus on the awesome majesty of God. "Do you not know? Have you not heard?" (verse 28, compare verse 21). Then in five staccato phrases he pointed the weary exiles back to their God, reminding them of the eternal truths that form the bedrock for all comfort during times of discouragement.

First, "the LORD is the everlasting God." "LORD" is the covenant name for God, often vocalized as *Yahweh*. Yahweh, the covenant-keeping God of Israel, is the *only* God of the universe; and He has existed for all eternity. Your problems, however large they may seem, only last for a short period of time. God existed before your problems began, and He will continue to exist long after your problems have vanished. And God has promised that a day is coming when you will leave behind this mortal body and enter the realm of immortality. It's much easier to face our problems when we remember that our souls will live forever, but our problems will not.

Second, God is "the Creator of the ends of the earth." God is not only eternal; He is also the One who fashioned all that is temporal. We helped our daughter, Becky, buy a new portable computer for Christmas. But when she started using it, the screen flickered on and off. By the second day it went completely dark. Obviously, something was wrong. We took the computer back to the store and they sent it off to their company's repair facility. They designed it, they built it, and they knew best how to fix it. In the same way, when we face problems and difficulties in our lives, we know we can share our burdens with the God who designed and built the world in which we live. You and I can trust Him with our problems because He knows how best to repair what He originally created.

Third, God "will not grow tired or weary." In popular culture God is often viewed as "the old man upstairs." The picture is usually that of a larger-than-life grandfather, complete with white hair and beard. But the God we can go to is not some tired grandfather who, having gotten the world started, somehow has let it slip beyond His grasp. When we face the hard times of life, we should remember that the God we run to is a God of unlimited power. He was, is, and always will be omnipotent. We know that we will never face a problem, difficulty, or obstacle that will be too difficult for Him to handle. We also know that we can run to Him today, tomorrow, next week, or next year and always find Him available and willing to assist. He will not grow weary of our constant cries for help.

Fourth, God's "understanding" is such that "no one can fathom." I can usually figure out small problems. Or at least I think I can. But far too often life becomes hopelessly complex. Like trying to help piece together Humpty Dumpty following his fall, the mess around me just seems too complex to ever fit together. But I know that I can go to a God in heaven who understands everything about life—every possible problem, every possible contingency, every possible solution, every possible effect, and every possible response. He knows the answer to all life's problems, and He has promised that "in all things" He "works for the good of those who love him, who have been called according to his purpose" (Romans 8:28). I can't possibly begin to figure out how He does that, but I'm so thankful that, as God, He does!

Fifth, God "gives strength to the weary and increases the power of the weak" (Isaiah 40:29). Where can you find the strength to walk life's rough roads? You won't find it in yourself but through the power that God Himself supplies. Perhaps the apostle Paul had this verse in mind when he wrote to the Christians at Philippi, "I can do everything through him who gives me strength" (Philippians 4:13).

When sorrow, pain, and loneliness invade our comfort zone, stripping away our façade of security and exposing our vulnerabilities, we are forced to ask and answer the cosmic questions of life. Is there a God? Does He care for us? Can He help us? Isaiah boldly proclaims that God *does* provide the strength and power we need to make it through life—and His supply is limitless!

Knowing in the Head . . . Trusting in the Heart

I know in my head these promises are true, but there have been times when I haven't felt the same in my heart. Several years ago I was invited to speak at a church, and I decided to speak on Isaiah 40. For whatever reason, the weekend just didn't unfold as I thought it ought. When I got home my wife asked how things went, and I blurted out, "It was a wasted weekend." Why did I feel like that? I don't know; I suppose it was because the response wasn't what I had expected. I just felt as if I had labored for nothing—that had the Sunday been scored as a baseball game I would have ended the day with "no hits, no runs, and no errors." I hadn't harmed God's kingdom program, but neither had I really done anything to move it forward.

And then God gave me a small glimpse of what He did with that weekend.

Four months after I spoke I received a letter from a member of that church. Her words made me feel so ashamed of my earlier self-pity and discouragement. She shared how God used that specific message to encourage her during a time of great personal loss. She wrote, "I want to thank you for the sermon you gave at my church one week after the funeral of my twelve-year-old son. I was not among the congregation [that day], but a friend gave me the cassette. I have listened to your words so often I have nearly memorized them."

At one point in the message I had used an illustration about a woman who had become so depressed and discouraged that she had taken her own life. That illustration spoke in a special way to this grieving mother. "I understand completely [her] feeling of hopelessness, and I know I will never have the answer to any of my 'whys.'"

She went on to explain the significance of my choice of Isaiah 40 and the impact of that message—at that specific time—on her life. "I am including a copy of my eulogy for my son, and you will see the importance to me of the text on which you spoke. More than once your words have brought me back from total despair and the very strong desire to leave this world. Thank you."

She was thanking me, but I was the one who needed to be thanking her. It was God who used the proclamation of His Word that Sunday morning. I felt as if I had failed, but He did something far beyond what I could ever have imagined. And then He graciously pulled back the veil and allowed me to see ever so slightly how He can use frail humans as the instruments of His grace. God let me be the instrument to encourage this grieving mother, and then He let her be the one to encourage me.

Are you struggling right now? Read once more verses 28–29. Focus on the wisdom, power, and understanding of God. He knows your need, and He will always be there to help. Then look for someone you can encourage. And as you encourage them, God will encourage you.

God's Power Unleashed

I know that the lamp beside my desk is connected to the Northern Indiana Public Service Company. The lamp cord is plugged into the wall socket that, ultimately, connects to the utility's large power generator in my region. I know all this, but until I turn on the switch, I'm still sitting in the dark! Knowledge alone isn't enough. It must be followed by action.

Isaiah has taken his readers on a journey of faith. Along the way he has used the Judean wilderness as the stage on which to display the unsurpassed power of God. God will *never* abandon His people. God can change the wilderness, which Isaiah used as a metaphor for problems that seem so permanent. Circumstances can change, much as the grass and flowers in the wilderness, but God's Word of promise will stand forever. All this is true because God has the sovereign might of a conquering hero and the gentle love of a tender shepherd. Compared to the power of God, every possible problem we face shrinks to insignificance. And God has promised to make His sustaining power available to us always. These are great truths, but they mean nothing if we don't respond! So how do we unleash God's power?

Isaiah first reminded his readers that not everyone takes advantage of God's resources for divine comfort and power. Some try to live life in their own strength, but even the best reach a point where their personal resources are exhausted. "Even youths grow tired and weary, and young men stumble and fall" (verse 30). Some may make it through life farther than others, but everyone eventually reaches a point where his or her strength gives out.

Isaiah has once again returned to the imagery of the wilderness. In this sunbaked land travelers tire quickly. Walking up and down the rock-covered hills is exhausting. The sun is relentless, places to find rest and refreshment all too few. The distance individuals can travel will vary. But unless they find shade and water, everyone will eventually collapse from exhaustion.

My favorite part of Israel is the wilderness. I love its stark beauty. In the Bible the wilderness was the place of testing. But it was also the location where people discovered the sufficiency of God's grace. It was the spot where living water gushed from rocks, manna arrived on the ground every morning, God appeared to His people in a cloud by day and a pillar of fire by night, a young shepherd boy discovered God's protection as he faced the lions and bears that menaced his small flock, and ravens brought food to a lonely prophet. The wilderness is where you learn how quickly your strength will vanish, and how breathtakingly awesome the God of the universe can become when you allow Him to supply that which you cannot supply yourself.

Having Hope

Having reminded his readers that human strength will eventually give out, Isaiah announced how to connect to God's never-ending source of strength and comfort. "But those who hope in the LORD will renew their strength" (verse 31a). The key word here is *hope*. In other versions of the Bible it is sometimes translated "wait." But what does it mean to hope in the Lord or to wait for Him? Our understanding of this word is crucial to the whole passage.

The Hebrew word literally means "to wait for" or "to look eagerly for" something. In Psalm 56:6 the word is used to describe the wicked who were intently and eagerly watching David, looking for an opportunity to kill him. "They conspire, they lurk, they *watch* my steps, eager to take my life" (italics added). This band of evildoers eagerly watched every step David took, anticipating the time when they would be able to act against him.

Isaiah calls on his readers to "eagerly watch for and wait on" the Lord. Dr. John Hartley provides a wonderful description of the action anticipated by this word. "The root means to wait or to look for with eager expectation. . . . Waiting with steadfast endurance is a great expression of faith. It means enduring patiently in confident hope that God will decisively act for the salvation of his people."[1]

Isaiah has brought us back to the essence of faith. Faith means we hope and wait upon God, anticipating His goodness and strength toward us. We do not have the physical resources to face all the problems life brings across our path. God has announced that He can supply the strength to sustain us through life, and He has promised to give us that strength if we only turn to Him to supply it. That choice is now ours—yours and mine.

We can continue to try to carry life's burdens in our own power, but each step we take further depletes our already meager supply of strength. The end of the journey is nowhere in sight, the ascent grows steeper, and we find our legs becoming heavier and less responsive.

Or we can stop, turn to God, and say, "Lord, I can no longer carry these burdens on my own. I believe You when You promised to bear my burdens and supply me with the strength and comfort I need to go on. I now eagerly look to You for that help. Please infuse me with Your strength and encourage me with Your comfort!"

After a full day of teaching, I returned home to learn my wife, Carol, had been on the phone with her dad's doctor in California. Dad had been found dead that morning at home in his bed. He had gone to sleep and had awakened in heaven! He would have been ninety in a couple of months.

As we rearranged our schedules to travel west, we attempted to contact our three children. Calls went to our two sons, but our thirty-three-year-old daughter, Joanne, who also lived in California, was not available. Several hours later we made contact with our son-in-law, Matt. He proceeded to inform us that late that same afternoon Joanne had suddenly collapsed, and all efforts to revive her had failed. Joanne was gone! We could not believe what we were hearing. Two heavy blows — deaths of two beloved family members on the same day!

Of all the questions that run through your mind at a time like that, the one that keeps coming back is Why? *Joanne and Matt had three little girls. They were involved in a new ministry in a church that was going very well.* Why, God? Why now? *It certainly did not seem fair, and it definitely was not right from our perspective.*

Our hearts were crushed. This was without a doubt the hardest thing Carol and I had ever experienced in our married life.

I do not know how the news spread, but our phone started ringing. Longtime friends called, one even from England, to express their love and to remind us of God's promises. Of course we had not lost our loved ones—we knew where they were. To be "absent from the

body" is to be "at home with the Lord" (2 Corinthians 5:8 NASB).
We were sorrowing, but not as "the rest who have no hope"
(1 Thessalonians 4:13 NASB).

A verse that came to mean a great deal to me during this
time is from the story of Jesus' encounter with Jairus in Mark 5.
Jairus asked Jesus to come heal his daughter. But before Jesus
could get to the house, the little girl died. Jesus, aware of the
girl's death, turned to Jairus and said, "Do not be afraid any
longer, only believe" (verse 36 NASB). Jesus' command could be
translated, "Keep on believing."

Jairus did believe in Jesus and in His power. That's why he
had come to ask for His help. Now what he needed to do was to
keep on believing. And that truth is what became my confidence
and hope. I believe the Lord is in control and that He has not only
accomplished His perfect plan in the lives of my father-in-law and
my daughter, but that He will continue to accomplish it in my life
as well.

Louis Barbieri, professor, department of theology
Moody Bible Institute, Chicago, Illinois

Postcards from the Wilderness

Isaiah's final image from the Judean wilderness is perhaps his best, because it visualizes what will take place when we turn to God and ask Him to unleash His sustaining power and comfort in our lives. Isaiah promised that those who do turn to God for His strength "will soar on wings like eagles; they will run and not grow weary, they will walk and not be faint" (verse 31b). I used to read this verse and imagine that God chose the image of the eagle because of its large, strong wings. Somehow I pictured the eagle flapping its wings in a way that provided extra power and lift, enabling it to keep flying when birds with lesser wings were forced to land. And then one day I saw an eagle flying over the Judean wilderness . . . and I understood why He chose this image!

The day was hot, and the sun was high in the sky. The group I was leading was standing on the edge of a major gorge in the wilderness. Off in the distance we could see small dust devils being stirred up by the wind. These funnel-shaped cones swirled skyward, being pulled aloft by the heat rising from the desert floor. As I glanced up at these dust devils, I saw a large eagle floating in the sky—wings outstretched and still! The eagle hovered effortlessly in the sky, making lazy circles over the barren wilderness. Every movement, every turn seemed to happen with absolute ease.

And then I realized the picture being painted by the prophet! To "soar on wings like eagles" is to be effortlessly borne aloft by a power you do not create. The image is *not* one that points to your power. Rather, it pictures a power that comes along beside and under you to lift you, hold you, sustain you. Eagles in the wilderness simply spread their wings and allow the wind to do all the work. And that "wind" for us is God's sustaining grace and power!

Shalom

So now, my friend, we are walking back from that magnificent vista of the Judean wilderness we just experienced together. Hopefully, the grandeur of the sight took your mind off your day-to-day struggles and helped you focus—if just for a short time—on the majesty and grace of our God. Perhaps you began your initial journey of faith as you read through these pages. Or perhaps you found a time of respite on your continuing journey of faith. In any event, it's now time for us to part company and continue on our separate paths.

Neither of us knows what lies just over the next hill. We might ascend to an unparalleled vista of joy and happiness. Or we might descend into a dark valley of sorrow and tears. But wherever life's pathway leads, I trust you will allow God to walk beside you on your journey. Remember His presence. Search out the promises in His Word. Develop a deeper personal relationship with Him. Seek His protection. And eagerly wait for, and hope in, His power. Let Him be the wind beneath the wings of your life . . . and learn to soar on wings like eagles!

The proper word for good-bye in Hebrew is "Shalom." Amazingly enough, it is also the word for "Hello." Literally, the word means "peace." It is intended almost as a blessing when greeting someone . . . or when saying farewell. And so, as you resume your journey through life, my prayer is that God's words of comfort from Isaiah 40 will walk beside you, and that God's peace will stand guard over your heart.

Shalom, my friend!

Acknowledgments

This book has been a dream of mine for many years. I want to extend a special word of thanks to those who helped make it a reality.

Mark Tobey, my thanks for your friendship . . . and your willingness to champion this book at Moody Publishers. I owe you much!

Jim Vincent, thank you for serving as editor for the project. Your skills are *greatly* appreciated . . . even when you asked the hard questions!

Danny Chookaszian, thank you for the picture of the eagle soaring over Israel. It might be stylized, but I trust you can still recognize that majestic bird we saw together.

Kathy, thank you for your incredible proofreading skills. After thirty years of marriage, I'm still in awe!

Notes

Chapter 1: Comfort Amid the Sand, Sweat, and Blood of Our Lives
   1. Psalm 23:4; John 14:2–3; Psalm 121:1–2 KJV.

Chapter 2: The Comfort of God's Presence
   1. George Frederic Handel, "Comfort Ye" and "Every Valley," public domain.
   2. Helen H. Lemmel, "Turn Your Eyes Upon Jesus," public domain.

Chapter 3: The Comfort of God's Promise
   1. Encyclopedia Smithsonian, s.v. "The Titanic," http://www.si.edu/resource/faq/nmah/titanic.htm.
   2. Of the 2,227 passengers, 68 percent (1,522 people) died in the sinking, according to the Encyclopedia Smithsonian.
   3. Letter from Moody Memorial Church to Walworth Road Baptist Church, London, collection 330, box 31, folder 9, archives of the Billy Graham Center, Wheaton College, Wheaton, Ill., http://www.wheaton.edu/bgc/archives/docs/titanic3.htm.

Chapter 4: The Comfort of God's Person
   1. Charles Weigle, "No One Ever Cared for Me Like Jesus." Copyright 1932, (administered by Singspiration Music (ASCAP). Brentwood-Benson Music Publishing, Inc.). All rights reserved. Used by permission.

Chapter 6: The Comfort of God's Power
   1. R. Laird Harris, Gleason L. Archer, Bruce K Waltke, *Theological Wordbook of the Old Testament*, vol. 2 (Chicago, Moody: 1980), s.v. "hwq," 791.

Other Books by Charles Dyer:

A Christian Travelers guide to the Holy Land
Essays in Honor of J. Dwight Pentecost
Integrity of Heart, Skillfulness of Hands
The Power of Personal Integrity
Prophecy in Light of today
The Rise of Babylon
Storm Clouds on the Horizon
Telescoping the Scriptures: Isaiah-Malachi
What's Next?
Who Owns the Land?
World News and Bible Prophecy

Since 1894, Moody Publishers has been dedicated to equip and motivate people to advance the cause of Christ by publishing evangelical Christian literature and other media for all ages, around the world. Because we are a ministry of the Moody Bible Institute of Chicago, a portion of the proceeds from the sale of this book go to train the next generation of Christian leaders.

If we may serve you in any way in your spiritual journey toward understanding Christ and the Christian life, please contact us at www.moodypublishers.com.

"All Scripture is God-breathed and is useful for teaching, rebuking, correcting and training in righteousness, so that the man of God may be thoroughly equipped for every good work."

—2 Timothy 3:16, 17

MOODY
PUBLISHERS

THE NAME YOU CAN TRUST®

A VOICE IN THE WILDERNESS TEAM

ACQUIRING EDITOR
Mark Tobey

COPY EDITOR
Jim Vincent

BACK COVER COPY
Anne Perdicaris

COVER DESIGN
Ragont Design

COVER PHOTO
Charles H. Dyer

INTERIOR DESIGN
Julia Ryan,
Designs By Julia
www.designsbyjulia.com

PRINTING AND BINDING
Color House Graphics

*The typeface for the text of this book is
Latin 725 BT*